Rooting Out Relationship Killers

Proven strategies to help you cultivate and maintain healthy relationships

Stephen Matthew

RIVER
PUBLISHING

River Publishing & Media Ltd
Barham Court
Teston
Maidstone
Kent
ME18 5BZ
United Kingdom

info@river-publishing.co.uk

ISBN 978-1-908393-29-6
Printed in the United Kingdom
Cover design by www.SpiffingCovers.com

Contents

What Others Are Saying...

"Nothing matters like relationships. In this practical book Stephen shares down-to-earth wisdom to help us protect, strengthen and restore them."
Rob Parsons, Founder and Chairman, Care for the Family.

"Every human being needs and desires healthy relationships. Everyone needs a relational environment where they can share and process life – a place where the ups and downs, the joys, excitement and the tragedies can be shared. Stephen Matthew's book will give you a biblical way of looking at relationships and will give you ideas to keep this important area of your life strong and healthy. It's a great read for everyone, regardless of your age or stage of life, as we all want meaningful and thriving relationships."
Pastor Gary Clarke, Lead Pastor, Hillsong Church London.

"This book is a gift to all who are seeking the wisdom to not just survive relationships, but to thrive within them. It flows from the pastoral heart of one of the most faithful and dedicated leaders we have had the privilege to share life with, as both a friend and fellow-leader. Stephen's relational investment has made our lives and churches all the richer. We recommend this book to every person: from married to single, young to old, and pastors to new believers. Within its pages are keys that will enable you

to enjoy the harvest only wise relational investments can bring, a harvest that will last for years to come."
Steve & Charlotte Gambill, Lead Pastors, LIFE Church UK.

"What an absolutely practical book, packed full of wisdom and insight on navigating, growing and strengthening the most important part of life - relationships. In this book Stephen identifies the many challenges, strains and mistakes that can so easily destroy relationships, and gives clear, proven and life-changing teaching that will transform your relationships and how you do life with others. Whether you need to see a relationship restored and reconciled or a healthy relationship become richer and stronger, this book gives you the tools to do it."
Clive Urquhart, Senior Leader, Kingdom Faith

"Steve's latest book is filled with helpful insights and wise observations of how to develop healthy relationships in all spheres of life. If read and acted upon, there is wisdom here to help many avoid the pain of broken relationships."
Stuart Bell, Senior Pastor, New Life Lincoln and Leader of the Ground Level Network.

Introduction

This is a book about relationships, the building blocks of our interpersonal lives. It is a positive book that will strengthen and enrich every relationship you have in life – both natural and spiritual – with the aim of keeping them healthy and strong.

My purpose in this book is to be both positive and preventative:

Positive in the sense that it majors on the positive aspects of relationship building, rather than being a book for people with major relationship dysfunction. It will, of course, help them, but I am not targeting them. This book is for everybody because we all have relationships and a deep desire to navigate them successfully. Somehow, we instinctively know that life will be better when we live it with others and have our life enriched by a matrix of great relationships.

Preventative in the sense that if you will take note of the relationship building advice in this book, major relationship dysfunction need never happen. That may sound like a bold claim, but I believe it with all my heart.

Relationships do not have to go wrong, be a constant nightmare to navigate or bring you nothing but heartache. They really can be the single greatest blessing in your life.

I do, of course, need to issue one rather obvious caveat, having made such a bold claim: The biggest problem with any relationship is the other person! We cannot act for them, think for them or relate for them. It does "take two to tango" as the saying goes. But where two or more people can agree on the fundamental relationship building principles we will explore in this book, the rewards can be life changing.

For this to be our experience, relationships have to be both understood and managed. We must understand the essential nature of relationships and, in particular, that God created us for relationship. It is, therefore, to the Creator's design that we will be looking for guidance as we explore how to mange our relationships successfully.

My approach is, therefore, unashamedly biblical and rooted in a strong conviction that God's way is the only way to build successful relationships, whether the people involved believe in him or not. These are divine, creation principles and apply universally to humanity, not just to those who call themselves Christian. But it is the Christians, of all people, who should be developing their relationships in line with their Creator, Saviour and Lord's design. We must never forget that our relationships are a crucial part of our witness. As Jesus said, *"Love one another. By this all men will know that you are my disciples"* (John 13:34-35). So, as we cultivate healthy relationships, we model the Creator's design for lonely, hurting humanity to see and emulate.

This book will do you good. It will make you a better friend, husband, wife, mother, father, brother, sister, team member, business partner, leader, manager or employee. As a result, your life will enrich those you relate to and do them good too. Everyone wins when we do relationships God's way!

So, thank you for making this positive investment into your relational world. My prayer is that it will equip you to enlarge your sphere of relationships, deepen your most significant ones and bring you the joy that can only come from having a wonderful matrix of healthy relationships.

Let's dig!

1
Made That Way

"Ping" went my mobile midway through the TV show. Nonchalantly, I glanced at the message. My gaze sharpened when I saw the sender – it was a friend I hadn't heard from for years. Now I was interested. But my heart soon sank. The message simply said their marriage seemed to be over and would I be willing to give them a listening ear.

Of course, the answer was "yes", but that message was a tipping point. It was actually the moment I realised I had to write this book.

For months prior to receiving that message I had been helping people navigate life, like all pastors do. But it seemed that every situation that came my way was a relationship breakdown. I had spent hours with businessmen in very serious strife with each other, who were about to take each other to court, married couples who were so estranged they couldn't say a single civil word to each other, and parents who were just one step away from disowning their children. And yes, they were all Christians.

For years I have had a reputation in some circles as being a man of harmony and peace, and it is true that I seem to have a grace from God to help bring disparate parties into unity. My position has always been simple: I just don't understand why people cannot get on together. Surely all it takes is humility, love and forgiveness? Maybe I'm just too simple! Yet, everywhere I turned there seemed to be relationship breakdown and dysfunction on a scale I had never quite seen before.

On and on it went. Then one day I noticed something else that troubled me. I observed that situations I had previously had grace to help resolve, I no longer seemed to have grace for. I was becoming tetchy and felt physically revolted at the thought of sitting in yet another relationship dispute. I'd had enough. For reasons I had yet to understand, that grace lifted from me. And it was the arrival of that text message which alerted me to it.

What was going on? Why was I being bombarded with tales of relational breakdown from what seemed like every quarter? And then I heard myself say to Kay, "Maybe God is trying to tell me something." He was. And now he had my full attention. One result from the ensuing process was this book.

I've spoken about relationships on and off for years and helped resolve many broken ones along the way, but never have I gathered my thoughts into a cohesive format in the way that this book has allowed me to. The process was enlightening, to say the least, and it totally reignited my belief that no relationship is ever beyond reconciliation if the parties are willing to work things through God's way.

But far more importantly, it affirmed to me that when relationships are developed correctly in the first place, they need never get into serious breakdown at all. This has become my overriding conviction when it comes to relationship dynamics and is the conviction behind this book.

The grace to help people in relational difficulties has returned to me too. But from now on I hope to be a dispenser of preventative relationship medicine, rather than a surgeon fighting to keep critically ill relationships alive. People with those important skills will always be needed, but my focus from now on will be to do all I can to reduce their workload. This book is part of that preventative medicine.

Don't fight it

Relationships are complex. The variables are myriad when two people embark on any kind of serious venture together, whether it is dating, starting a business together or joining a church. In fact, the stated purpose of the relationship becomes irrelevant at one level; what matters far more is the personality, character, motives, temperament, world-view and plain quirkiness of the individuals concerned. Their union, friendship, partnership or however you describe it, will probably succeed or fail depending on how well they navigate their interpersonal complexities, not on whether they both want the same end result.

It is those same complexities that lead some people to withdraw from meaningful relationships altogether; they become isolate, independent and detached. Not a happy place to be, but from their perspective the lesser of two evils. As the saying goes, "People: can't live with them; can't live without them". We all know the feeling.

But if we are honest, the majority of us would rather have relationships than be alone, even if they are hard work. Why is that? The simple answer is that God made us that way. So fighting the urge to develop great relationships is actually unnatural. Whether you like it or not, God created you to be social. You have a deep, in-built need for healthy relationships – which is probably at the root of why you are reading this book!

Just think about our origins for a moment. Genesis chapter 1 teaches us that God created this wonderful world, placed Adam in it and declared it to be fundamentally good. But in chapter 2 we discover that in that sin-free, newly created, pristine environment, something was *not* good and had to be fixed. We read:

"The Lord God said, 'It is not good for the man to be alone.'" (Genesis 2:18).

His response was to make the woman, Eve, and only then was the day declared to be "very good".

God could have made the man and the woman at the same time but he chose not to. I believe he did this deliberately to teach us a fundamental relationship lesson that is rooted in the way he has created us. The point being that God made us to be social beings. We are made for relationships. Without them we are "not good" and destined to live an unhappy, unfulfilled and unfruitful life. We need other people; it is just the way God made us.

What's more, God created us to be just like him. We are made *"in his image"* (Genesis 1:27). God is not an isolate being; he exists as the godhead, a trinity of God the father, God the Spirit and God the Son. The Triune nature of God is not something people have invented, it is the way God has revealed himself to be – it is actually so hard to grasp I don't think our limited human minds could ever have thought it up! It is a vast and glorious concept. He has revealed himself to be a social God and created us in his image. That is why we need other people. It is an intrinsic part of our being.

I think that's also why God goes on to say something helpful about every imaginable kind of relationship in the Bible. So, making a conscious decision to develop great social skills works with your creative make-up rather than against it.

I am not saying it will therefore be easy! People are complex, after all. But I am saying that personal fulfilment and happiness always includes having great relationships. And for that reason the price of developing those relationships is always worth paying. It cost Adam a rib to find his ideal relationship partner. For you and me it is more likely to cost us our pride, our willingness to be honest or the price of dismantling the walls we have constructed to keep people at arm's length from us. We have to give something of ourselves away. That's the cost.

So I must deal with anything that stops me relating to you properly. I may need to change my preconceived ideas about you, destroy the "box" I had you in, get over the fact that you once let me down, forgive you, or even repay you for wrongs I did to you. For our relationship to thrive, it will cost us both. But the value it will add to our lives is priceless.

First understand, then, that God has made you social. Your need for healthy, life-enriching relationships is simply an expression of the way you are made. So, don't fight it, work with it. Don't let the cost or the challenge put you off, because to do so will violate the way God has made you. The prize is worth any short-term pain because healthy relationships enrich your life like nothing else in this world.

The lead

God has not only made us social beings, he also created us as spiritual beings. You are spiritual. By that I am not referring to anything you do, but to what you are – your essential being. And this also plays a key part in understanding how to cultivate great relationships as a Christian.

Your personal relationship with God began the moment you became a Christian. You are no longer spiritually dead but alive. You are now spirit, soul and body working together in harmony; all the elements of your creative make-up functioning as God intended. And only now – as a whole person – can you truly build healthy relationships with the rest of the created order.

Now that you are spiritually alive, God's Spirit in you takes the lead. Remember, you made him "Lord" which means boss. So the way you developed and handled relationships before becoming a Christian has to change. They were previously informed and led by what your body and soul dictated; by your mind, will, emotions and bodily feelings. But because God's Spirit now leads the way, you start to build relationships in the way the Creator teaches us to. That not only gives us hope, it paves the way for the most successful and fulfilling human relationships possible.

You must settle this now. You need a healthy relationship with God to inform and direct all other human relationships. It is that fundamental. God made us social beings, so we need each other for a happy and fulfilling life. And God made us spiritual beings, so we need to allow our God-directed spirituality to set the pace in how we conduct and develop those relationships.

Whenever a Christian decides to develop a human relationship in a way that goes against the way God teaches, they struggle. In fact, many times they suffer too. As a consequence they can become hurt, bitter and confused. Christian marriages can fail, Christian business people can fall out, and Christian children can live in poor relationships with their parents. But this is never God's intention.

God has given us a wonderful set of relationship-building principles in the Bible and his Holy Spirit to help us apply them in our day-to-day lives. All we have to do is choose to do it his way, which may seem a hard choice at the time. But because God is good, knows the future and is fundamentally "for" us, as we trust his word and take simple steps of obedient faith, our relationships become progressively healthier. Before long, we are living out God's creative purpose by being spiritual people who know how to enjoy the healthy relationships he created us for.

I suspect you are reading this book because you instinctively know that God has made you a social being and you want to get better at doing relationships. That is good. But the process must also fully embrace your spirituality to be the best it can be.

So, make a strong decision not to fight the way God has made you. Then commit to building every relationship you have according to the Creator's pattern. This will ensure we are all on the same page as we begin to explore this theme together.

2
Relationship Gardening

A gardening buddy of mine was among the people I supported in the period leading up to the writing of this book. He had been in what appeared to be a stable and happy marriage for nearly 20 years. As the children got older his wife returned to work where she found a whole new lease of life. The confidence she gained also gave her the courage to speak up about the dysfunction in their relationship. She accused him of driving the children away by his overbearing attitude and of having treated her like a chattel behind closed doors all their married life. His pride prevented him acknowledging anything was wrong and she eventually left him.

Some time later he broke. He and God did some serious business and part of his restoration was admitting she had been right about his behaviour. One day we were sat in his garden discussing it all and he made the point that the "seeds" of his wrong-doing had been present in the soil of their relationship for the whole of their married life. But when they sprang to life, he had simply been too proud to ask for help. So the dormant killers in the soil of their relationship were allowed to take root, flourish and choke the life out of it.

That conversation got me thinking because I love gardening and suspect Jesus did too! Not everyone may agree, but you cannot get away from the fact that Jesus used many farming and gardening illustrations to help people understand his message. He told parables about sowing seed in a range of soils, the problems of planting wheat and weeds together, the progress of a mustard seed, the attitude of workers in a vineyard and the issues faced by farmers who have an over-supply of crops. He even likened himself to a grapevine.

These images were, of course, drawn from the every day lives of his listeners. Their society was rural rather than urban for the most part, and these stories became simple, accessible vehicles through which to communicate profound, life-changing truth. And I am going to borrow one to illustrate the rest of this book. So if you are a gardener, you will immediately get this. If not, let me explain.

One of Jesus' earliest parables was about a field that contained four kinds of soil, something every gardener has to grapple with. The farmer decided to sow seed across the whole field. He did not concentrate just on the areas he thought were more fertile, he was generous and indiscriminate. The seed went everywhere. But, of course, the success of the seed depended entirely on the ground it landed in. We read:

"As he was scattering the seed, some fell along the path, and the birds came and ate it up. Some fell on rocky places, where it did not have much soil. It sprang up quickly, because the soil was shallow. But when the sun came up, the plants were scorched, and they withered because they had no root. Other seed fell

among thorns, which grew up and choked the plants. Still other seed fell on good soil, where it produced a crop – a hundred, sixty or thirty times what was sown." (Matthew 13:3-8)

Even without further explanation it is not difficult to understand what Jesus was trying to communicate. The simple truth is that everything hinges on the fertility of the soil, not the seed. The seed has life in itself, all it needs is the correct growing conditions. But to help his disciples at the time, Jesus did explain it further:

"Listen then to what the parable of the sower means: When anyone hears the message about the kingdom and does not understand it, the evil one comes and snatches away what was sown in his heart. This is the seed sown along the path. The one who received the seed that fell on rocky places is the man who hears the word and at once receives it with joy. But since he has no root, he lasts only a short time. When trouble or persecution comes because of the word, he quickly falls away. The one who received the seed that fell among the thorns is the man who hears the word, but the worries of this life and the deceitfulness of wealth choke it, making it unfruitful. But the one who received the seed that fell on good soil is the man who hears the word and understands it. He produces a crop, yielding a hundred, sixty or thirty times what was sown." (Matthew 13:18-23)

First notice how Jesus describes the seed. It is *"the message about the kingdom"* (v19). The kingdom of God is the sphere of God's rule; the seed represented any message about that. The seed is, therefore, a picture of every message – whether written, spoken, sung, acted, mimed, preached, taught or chatted – that teaches us how to live under God's rule as his people.

It was the "message of the kingdom" that we responded to when we first became a Christian. We gladly made Jesus Lord, bowed the knee to his kingship and chose to live his way. And it is the message of the kingdom we hear every time God speaks to us through the Bible or by his Holy Spirit in our hearts, whatever format that truth was communicated in.

When God speaks, it is the King speaking. So if we want to thrive as his subjects we must become like the fertile soil in this parable. We must receive the "seed" of God's word, water it, keep it free of weeds and stones so that it develops strong roots and, in due course, produce a wonderful harvest.

The success of God's word is always related to the human response to it. That is the importance of this parable. God does not act in spite of us, he acts with us and through us. Everything about the Christian life is relational. We live by faith (Romans 1:17) and faith is a relational process of hearing God's word and doing it – faith and actions working together.

God's word – the seed – will not "return to him empty" according to Isaiah (55:11); it will always "accomplish the purpose for which it was sent". But sometimes it has to wait. That is because God, the farmer, has chosen to work with us in relationship and not irrespective of us. He waits until the soil is ready to work with the seed. And sometimes that is a very long time.

That is exactly what happened when Old Testament Israel entered the Promised Land. God had repeatedly spoken to them and promised it was theirs for the taking. But they still had to take it. They had to believe God's word – the seed – and live in the light of it. If they did, the fruit promised would be theirs.

Sadly, the first generation who received all this "seed" chose to believe the negative report of the spies and failed to go in (Numbers 13).

So God waited. The seed remained in tact. The promises were still true. All it needed was a people who would be like "fertile soil" and receive the "message of the kingdom" and be obedient to it. Joshua's generation eventually became that people and what an amazing time they had advancing as God's people! But how sad that many of God's people died before ever experiencing what God promised them, simply because they refused to believe and act on God's word. They were hard ground, like the seed that fell on the path.

I say all this to help you understand a very important principle when it comes to our theme of cultivating healthy relationships. The King has a lot to say about relationships. There is, therefore, a lot of relationship "seed" in the Bible and we will talk about some of it. But it is a total waste of time unless you are willing to be like the fertile soil. Without an attitude that fully embraces what God says about how to have healthy relationships you are in danger of being like that generation who never entered the Promised Land. As a Christian you have a "promised life", a brand new start, a hope and a future. Living it to the full demands that you submit to the wonderful, benevolent rule of your king, Jesus.

That is the underlying challenge of this book. We all want healthy relationships, but are we willing to receive the "message of the kingdom" as it speaks into how we handle them? It will take bold decisions, hard work and the wisdom to make good choices. But the fruit will be worth it.

I pray we will all say "yes" to the "message of the kingdom" about relationships and so experience the joy and fulfilment that comes from having a wide range of happy, healthy and fruitful relationships.

The weeds

Our resolve, then, is to be like the fertile soil in this parable. Now let me explain one more thing that emerges from it.

The problem with fertile soil is that everything grows in it. So whilst we concentrate on nurturing the good seeds we specifically planted, weeds always seem to emerge alongside them. As a result, weeding becomes a normal and necessary part of good gardening – the bit we hate!

I mean, we never deliberately sowed the weeds, they just appeared. Birds may have put them there or the wind carried them to our soil. All we know is that they need to be pulled up as soon as they are spotted because, as Jesus described, they will *"choke it, making it unfruitful"* (v22).

This is the image I want you to grasp as we get practical. Because we are committed to being fertile soil we must always have an eye out for random weeds that may start to take root in the fertile soil of our healthy relationships. If left unattended, those little weeds will slowly strangle and choke the healthy relationships we are growing. It can be very subtle, gradual and seemingly painless to start with. But eventually we will pay the price of not rooting out those little weeds if we do not keep an eye on them.

This is my fundamental approach in the next few chapters. We will be weed spotting, but in a positive context. We will be looking for little weeds in fertile soil and learning how to deal with them in good time, so that they never have the chance to develop and undermine a given relationship. We will be rooting out the potential relationship killers.

One final cautionary image to put in your mind before moving on. Before entering full-time Christian ministry over thirty years ago, I practiced as a Chartered Building Surveyor and I still love building and buildings. When conducting general surveys or carrying out specific building fault analysis, one of the regular things we are mindful of is root damage. Over the years I have seen walls, drains and even whole buildings undermined by a large root that was simply left unattended for many years.

It is shocking but true: a small weed, just a tiny root, can totally undermine and crack a large building if left unattended for long enough. And the same can happen to a relationship. If the little "weed" of a relationship killer is not removed in good time, it has the potential to undermine, crack and completely destabilise the "building" of the relationship.

Our aim, then, is to identify and root out any little weeds in the fertile soil of our healthy relationships which, if left unattended, will choke them, making them unfruitful. Always being mindful that if we allow them to grow unattended for long enough, they have the potential to eventually cause the building to crack or even collapse.

By doing this, we are rooting out the seeds of potential separation well before they can ever lead to divorce in a marriage, the acrimonious dissolution of a business partnership, children leaving home and never returning, or people leaving a team or church in bitterness and bad attitude.

Weeding and Feeding

I believe the nasty little weeds we will now identify and explore together affect all our relationships – the full range, from casual acquaintances to our life-partners. But they do have increasing importance the closer the nature of the relationship they take root in. So, married people in particular, get your gardening gloves on!

Getting your spiritual garden fork out to remove any weeds that, if left alone, would slowly damage your healthy relationships is both *positive* and *preventative*. But, on its own, it is still just a little bit too focussed on the problems for my liking. Yes, we must be "weed conscious" and have an eye out for their nasty little green shoots as part of our regular relationship maintenance. But alongside the weeding we must also be proactively doing things to maintain and enrich the soil of our relationships. We must be *feeding* it.

Good relationships, like good soil, need fertiliser and nutrients adding to replace the ones taken by the vigorously growing plants. Many a weed takes root simply because the soil has been neglected. So a good gardener gets busy maintaining the quality of his soil by adding nutrients to it. This promotes healthy growth. Likewise, for us, we must add positive relationship-building principles and practices to the soil of our relationships if they are to thrive and be fruitful.

A relationship is a living thing, just like a plant. It is organic. It goes through seasons, is affected by a range of external factors, but has within it the potential to be healthy and fruitful if conditions are right. That is why we must both "weed and feed" every relationship we have. They cannot be left alone, taken for granted or left to their own devices. When they are, weeds quickly spring up around them and the nutrients that once sustained them become exhausted. It is a double blow to their health. They become stunted in their growth, bear little fruit, become unable to resist attacks from diseases or pests, and eventually wither and die.

I have seen too many marriages like that and it saddens me deeply. The once thriving relationship has become decimated by a failure to control the weeds and to add regular nutrients. Both are needed. Family, church and business relationships can all go the same way if we do not remain active as "relationship gardeners".

What follows is a look at some of the more common and persistent relationship weeds we need to be looking out for. But more importantly, we will also identify specific *relationship feeds* that will counteract each one by adding positive strength to the growing relationship.

So, get your spiritual gardening gloves on and lets root out those relationship killers.

3
Together

At the centre of every relationship is a presupposition that we will do things together.

In a marriage, husband and wife embark on a journey of togetherness and shared lives. Church is an exercise in community life at a whole range of levels. A friendship is wonderful because of the things you do and share together, the energy and encouragement that flows from one to the other, and the understanding that you can achieve more together than on your own. Business partners bring complimentary expertise and acumen to the working relationship that bring greater rewards than sole trading. And so we could go on.

At the core of every healthy relationship is togetherness, teamwork and shared life. In a word, they are a partnership.

But over time, people and relationships change. Initial intentions can get lost in the busyness of the developing relationship and personal agendas can shift. It becomes all too easy to simply forget that this relationship is actually a partnership.

When this happens, it is like a small weed taking root in the fertile soil of the relationship. That weed is called independence and once the weed of independence starts to grow, there will be trouble ahead! That's because independence is an attitude that fundamentally works against the relationship. It takes unilateral decisions without considering their impact on the relationship and thus, slowly chokes it.

Independent attitudes in any relationship must, therefore, be spotted early and addressed by doing some relationship weeding. That requires proactive intervention by you, the relationship gardener in this scenario.

However, as all good gardeners know, prevention is always better than the hard work required to dig out well established weeds. So they regularly add nutrients and other elements to the soil to keep weed growth down. In this case, the best possible relationship "feed" you can add to the soil of a relationship is to regularly affirm your commitment to partnership.

A commitment to healthy partnership keeps the weed of independence at bay. That simply means having a commitment to the bigger reason you entered the relationship in the first place than to your personal desires.

The fact is, two people can be married but not be true partners. They live under the same roof, share finances and a common surname. But in practice they are living independent lives. He has his friends, she has hers. He plays golf, she goes to the gym. He has his career, she has hers. He likes to boast that he "does what he wants" and isn't tied to her apron strings. She loves to play the "independent woman" card and assure her friends that she is not "under his thumb". As time passes their independent choices slowly pull them apart until, one day, the bond is severed. He or she makes one independent choice too many and it becomes a defining issue. The marriage is over. That is a tragedy and one that could have been avoided by keeping their commitment to partnership alive.

Similarly, two people can enter a business relationship but over time develop totally different agendas. What started as a mutual partnership becomes strained by competing personal ambitions, motives and unilateral decision making. They become partners in name only. In practice they are each doing their own independent thing and are destined to separate.

In the same way, people can join a church, ministry team or sports team and never become a true partner. What always flags the problem up is a tendency to be independent, act unilaterally, do their own thing or simply be inconsiderate.

This may seem at first glance to be just a little weed. But for a marriage to succeed, a business partnership to thrive and a church experience to be truly life-enriching, independence must die.

Individuality

"Hold on there," I hear some of you saying. "Aren't we supposed to be true to ourselves as individual human beings?" And the answer is always "Yes". So, let me make an important distinction here. Independence is bad, it ruins a relationship. But individuality is good, it enriches a relationship.

We are each a unique individual, made in God's image and with a distinct set of life-skills, experiences, interests and abilities.

That is your individuality, your personhood, who you are.

Your individuality complements your relationships. From it, you bring strength to the relationship, but it must be outworked within a commitment to partnership if the relationship is to thrive and remain healthy.

In a healthy partnership, it is not "all about me" and it is not "all about you". It is not *my* money it is *our* money. These are not *my* children they are *our* children. It is *our* house, *our* car, *our* holiday, *our* church ... you get my point!

Your commitment to partnership means you will always consider the other person. Late one summer afternoon a few of my friends and I spent a leisurely couple of hours playing nine holes of golf. Very pleasant. While we were enjoying a drink in the clubhouse before returning home, someone suggested we stay out and eat together. "Great idea," we all said.

Then the phone calls started. A few of us were married so needed to let our partners know we would be home later than expected. But it was also then that the banter started! One friend withdrew from the group to chat to his wife, only to be barraged with comments from the single guys like, "Just ringing for permission?" "I thought you wore the pants in your house!" and so on.

All good natured banter you would have thought, but my friend was rightly unimpressed. "No," he replied. "I'm not asking for permission, I'm just being considerate. There's more than just me to think about." I appreciated his sentiment.

I have a pretty busy diary that sometimes takes me away from home for overnight stays. But I am married and do not want to make independent decisions about my movements without involving my wife, Kay. The cynical, macho-men may see it as me "asking for permission", but I am committed to the partnership we enjoy. So getting the diary out and making choices about when to stay home or be away is about cooperation, coordination and consideration. It is about partnership.

Commitment to partnership means thinking for two – or however many there are in the relationship group. If you are on the team, it spoils it for everyone if you don't turn up; you let the whole side down. As a husband and father I had to get used to thinking for six – having four children! And it was sometimes so hard when my independent desires seemed to be frustrated because of the needs of the family or other family members' preferences. At times like that we have to take a step back and focus again on the reason we are together.

Remember, the shared goal is greater than the personal one, that is why you are in this relationship. So if needed, step aside, lay your independent desire down and cheer your partners on. Because if it is a true partnership, you will share in their glory too!

Independence must not be allowed to take root in a partnership. If one person's will is imposed on the other, you will have problems. Equally, if one person's will is exercised without reference to the other, you will have problems.

So, if the weed of independence begins to spring up, pull it out fast. But more importantly, keep it at bay by feeding your relationships with a regular dose of affirming your commitment to partnership. As the Scripture says, *"Two are better than one"* for very many reasons (Ecclesiastes 4:9).

And if you are not willing to be a partner, share your life

with others, or give something of yourself away for the joy of achieving a shared goal, spare a thought for others and stay single!

The Weed: Independence

The Feed: Commitment to Partnership

4
Whole

We all carry the marks of our life-so-far and some of those marks have left us damaged. We bear mental, emotional, spiritual and relational scars whether we like it or not. Some, we have been healed from, others we are in a process of recovery from and others are sometimes suppressed deep within our soul where people can never see them.

Damage can also be inflicted on us from our current relationships. If they become unhealthy, we may say or do things to one another that leave lasting scars, hurt or wounds.

Whatever your history, the fact is that you bring any such wounds from the past into every new relationship you start unless you have completed a process of recovery and healing. Left unattended, old hurts, grudges, attitudes and patterns of dealing with certain issues will eventually reappear, just like a little weed – the weed of past wounds – and they will choke the new relationship.

So, you will get busy if you are determined not to let your past mess up your future and root this troublesome weed out. But in addition, because you see a positive future for the relationship, you will feed its relational soil with a feed designed to keep this weed at bay. That feed is a commitment to personal health and wholeness.

A marriage situation we spoke into some time ago eventually revealed that the wife had past wounds from a series of negative encounters with men. To use her words, "I just don't trust men." It had been suppressed deeply but the little weed had now sprouted in the soil of their relationship and had to be dealt with. Unless she allowed that wound to be exposed and healed, her husband had no chance!

Thankfully, for the sake of their partnership, she committed to a process that brought wholeness and the weed of past wounds was removed. But, it was their ongoing mutual commitment to each be personally healthy, at every level, that caused their marriage to flourish.

Not too long ago a concerned fiancée confided in me that her husband-to-be had "a bit of a temper". "I'm sure it's just the stress of the wedding," she added. I probed a little and discovered he was actually prone to fairly regular angry outbursts and she was a little frightened by them.

Her final comment was, "I'm sure he will be fine once we are married."

"Oh no he won't," I had to tell her. "He is on his best behaviour right now!" She was shocked by my response, but it is true. All guys are on their best behaviour in the lead up to the wedding, so if any little weeds of concern appear then, they must be addressed fast. If those weeds relate to serious past wounds they can become serious detractors from the healthy development of the relationship.

In that particular situation we "had a chat" and it transpired he had such a deep-seated anger management problem that they decided to postpone the wedding for six months while they worked on their personal health. Today they are happily married and all the stronger for their commitment to personal health and wholeness.

So, we deal with the potential damage cause by past wounds by making a commitment to personal health and wholeness. That means understanding what "wellness" looks like and taking steps to become it. By so doing, you give the gift of a "healthy you" to your partner in the relationship.

Healthy people are easy to talk to. They don't bully, threaten or intimidate their spouse, business associates or fellow church members. They don't get defensive, lash out in anger or clam up creating uncomfortable silences.

Healthy people are secure. They do not need constant assurance. They don't manipulate people emotionally, sexually or financially to get the assurance they crave. They are secure in who they are.

Healthy people get help when they need it. They are not too proud to admit they don't know what to do in a situation or ask for help. They are teachable and wisdom is eagerly sought from those with more experience about their situation. What they learn they are then quick to apply for the benefit of everyone in the relationship.

Healthy people respect themselves. They value their God-given abilities, body, personality and make up. They do not harm themselves, damage their bodies or try to escape from themselves through alcohol, drugs or other mind-altering substances. They have learned to love the way God has made them.

Healthy people respect others. They do not demand you become like them, but appreciate your uniqueness as an individual and celebrate it. They are happy when you do better than them. They encourage and cheer you on, and take appropriate pleasure in the privilege of being your friend, colleague or partner.

Healthy people are open. They are not a "closed book", hard to understand or emotionally detached from those closest to them. They are open and honest about their mistakes, the lessons they have learned from them and happy to help others not make the same ones.

Healthy people are balanced. They avoid emotional, spiritual and physical extremes because they have often learned the hard way to maintain an appropriate friends-family-work-leisure-church-private life balance.

Finally, please remember that this is a commitment to work on yourself, not your partner! They must be released to work their own process and you must work yours.

Give one another the gift of permission to get help if you need it. Never hold it against each other and concentrate on healing your own wounds.

Let your attitude be: Because I love you, I will be the best I can for you, and get the help I need when I need it.

The fact is, you can never make enough positive changes to make a wounded person happy. They need their own healing.

Let's make a commitment, therefore, to being personally healthy – emotionally, spiritually, behaviourally and physically –

and so ensure the soil of our relationships is kept free from the pernicious weed of past wounds.

The weed: Wounds of the past
The feed: Personal health and wholeness

5
Understood

Silence is the lowest form of communication.

Some would say that to call silence communication is a contradiction in terms. But we all know that in a relationship context, a silence is usually saying something. And silence can be deafening!

Can we be clear: whenever there is a silence, there is never "nothing wrong". You know how it goes. The silence is screaming at you, "There is something wrong". So you enquire, "What's wrong?" only to be told, "Nothing." So now you know they are telling lies!

What come next is where the relationship weed of silence begins to kill the relationship. In the void caused by the silence, conspiracy theories are incubated, fear takes root and insecurities deepen. We are left thinking things like, "What have I done wrong?" "I wonder if he is thinking of leaving me?" "What is she thinking about me now?" It could be absolutely anything. And the sad fact is that however you answer the question to yourself, it will be wrong! But in the silence, your wrong conclusion festers, grows and chokes the relationship.

Without clear communication you will never understand what is going on inside the head of a person who has chosen to communicate something through silence. Conflicts are never resolved by silence and a person's true motive never understood. That is why silence is a relationship killer. It is a devastating weed that quickly restricts the growth of any relationship.

Relationships always benefit from a good dose of communication. In fact, relationships thrive on good communication. They are enriched by the exchange of information, ideas and emotions expressed between the parties. Good communication is therefore a nutrient, a relationship feed that must be added consistently to the soil of our healthy relationships.

A commitment to open communication will keep the weed of silence at bay. Not long after Kay and I were married she started disappearing upstairs and sitting quietly in the bedroom where she liked to read. It was never announced, she just went. Being an insecure young man I pondered what was going on. Had I done something wrong? I mean, we are supposed to do everything together now we are married, aren't we? Before long the lack of explanation – the silence – had me incubating all manner of silly outcomes. So I tentatively enquired and a discussion ensued. We communicated. She needed space from me from time to time – space to think, read, pray and be at peace with herself. Ah! Now I understood, stopped fretting and soon learned that when she had her space, she was a better person for it and our relationship was enriched.

That example was not even about the deliberate use of silence to communicate something, it was just something we had not talked about before. We quickly learned that it is best to talk about everything and not leave unhelpful silences for conspiracy theories to breed in. This took us into deeper levels of communication, something all relationships need to grasp.

By definition, communication is "a process of sharing information with another person in such a way that they understand what you are saying". That process involves speaking, listening, body language, expressions and touch, but always with the aim of being properly understood.

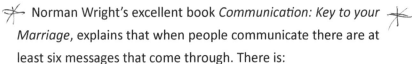 Norman Wright's excellent book *Communication: Key to your Marriage*, explains that when people communicate there are at least six messages that come through. There is:

- What you mean to say
- What you actually say
- What the other person hears
- What the other person thinks they hear
- What the other person says about what you said
- What you think the other person said about what you said

No wonder we misunderstand each other sometimes! But this shows just how important it is that we work on our communication to ensure it is clear.

To this, add the personal weaknesses or hang-ups we each may have about communicating. Some have simply never learned how to talk or open up to other people. Others are fearful of exposing what they think or feel, for fear of being hurt or rejected. Some even have such a low self-image that they don't believe they have anything to offer, so stay silent.

All this takes work to overcome — the work of feeding your relationship soil with the wonderful nutrient of good communication. As you work on it, you will discover the relationship deepens. Your relationship is only ever as deep as your willingness to communicate with absolute openness and clarity.

I'm sure you have noticed how people communicate at different levels. For example:

Some communicate only in **clichés**. They go no deeper than, "Hi there!" "How are you today?" "Fine thanks." "Pity about the weather!" This is very safe communication, as it gives nothing of their real thoughts or feelings away.

Others go a step deeper and are happy to **report facts about others**. Things like, "Joe tells me Sheila's pregnant again." "Oh, that reminds me, the dog's going to have pups again!" Again, this is safe as it only talks about others and includes no personal opinions or expression of personal feelings.

One step deeper is where I would say true communication begins. Here, we become willing to **share some of our ideas and judgments.** We step out of ourselves and risk sharing personal ideas. We explain our reasons for making specific decisions and doing certain things. We say things like, "I've decided to look for a part-time job because we need the extra cash to afford a bigger car to get all the children in."

A fourth step deeper is to then be willing to **communicate our feelings and emotions** about the facts, ideas, judgments and decisions. So now we may be saying, "I just cannot stand another long journey with the kids all cramped up in that little car! We have to get something bigger or they'll drive me crazy.

So, I've decided to do something about it and look for a part-time job which should allow us to afford a bigger one."

Finally, we get to what can only be called **completely open communication**. Here we enjoy absolute honesty between us. It is very special and a most powerful feed for the relationship, ensuring its health and productivity. All marriages should aim for this. Other relationships should be conducted at a depth that is appropriate for them.

So, communication is the feed that counteracts the weed of silence.

Communication is a large subject and one worth exploring more if silence is a particularly prevalent weed in your relationship soil. But, at the very least, please commit to developing good communication by ensuring it is the following three things:

Communication should be CLEAR

Use clear language, ask questions to clarify things and allow time for each other to process the words spoken. Never use hints – they are easily misunderstood or missed altogether. Say what you mean and work hard to say it in the way you want it to be received.

Communication should be CONTROLLED

You will never communicate properly when emotions are out of control. So pick your moment. Create space to talk when you are calm, there is time to explain things properly and when things have less chance of coming across wrongly.

I know you cannot always wait! But you can always work hard to keep volatile emotions under control which may otherwise impede the clarity of the communication.

Communication should be CONSTRUCTIVE

Communicate positively by focussing on the good things about the other person. Don't focus on the negative qualities but be constructive, even if you are dealing with a negative situation. Your tongue has *"the power of life or death"* according to the Bible (Proverbs 18:21). So use it to bring life to your relationships.

The Weed: Silence
The Feed: Communication

6
Faithful

Trust is the bonding agent of every relationship. It is relationship glue.

The depth and strength of a relationship is inextricably linked to the trust between the people in it. As trust builds, so does the relationship. As trust declines, so does the relationship. It is that simple.

That is why Jesus taught us to be trustworthy in dealing with everyone. He modelled transparent honesty in all his relationships and encouraged us to do the same by letting "our yes be yes and our no be no" (Matthew 5:37).

The fact is, we enter every relationship with a measure of mistrust. We are not sure how far we can trust the other person nor how far they are actually trusting us. But gradually, as the relationship deepens and we get to know each other better, mistrust is replaced by trust, and it establishes itself at a level appropriate for the relationship.

Trust can, therefore, take a long time to build, especially if we have been let down by people before. That's why we must protect it once we have it and work hard to do nothing that would undermine people's trust in us.

We must, therefore, be ruthless with the smallest weed of mistrust that pops up in our relationship soil, because it is one of the most difficult ones to eradicate if it is allowed to develop a strong root.

Every small lie, little deception or half-truth is a little weed of mistrust. And their roots quickly spread and become more entangled if allowed to continue unchecked. I believe that where the weed of mistrust takes significant root, we are potentially always just one lie away from its root seriously cracking the building of our relationship.

For example, maybe you have a friend that your partner does not really like you spending time with. One evening you are with that particular friend and your partner rings, so you lie about who you are with – you just don't want the hassle of explaining it all again and the grief it brings into your relationship. Then some time later they find out. Ouch! Now what? Well, you are probably going to play it down, blag your way through and try to keep everything tickety-boo. They, however, are not asking themselves, "Why did they lie to me?" They are asking the bigger question of, "If they lied about that, what else have they lied to me about?" And the weed of mistrust chokes a bit more life out of the once healthy relationship.

We all hate the negative atmosphere mistrust creates. The "walking on egg-shells", the suspicion, the seemingly never-ending need to explain our movements, spending decisions or motives. We just long to trust and be trusted again. So how do we do it?

The weed of mistrust has only one remedy, it must be rooted

out of the relationship by adding copious amounts of the feed called "being trustworthy". It is the only feed that will truly kill this weed and keep it at bay once eradicated. Be trustworthy.

However, there are a few "products" out there which may look like they will solve your mistrust problem. They may even promise to, but they are faulty goods – they cannot be trusted for this task! Those so-called remedies for mistrust are *promises*, *love* and *forgiveness* – all much-needed relationship elements. But none are able to suppress the weed of mistrust like being trustworthy can. Let me explain.

It is not a "promise" issue. The answer to mistrust is not found in promising, "I will never to do it again" or "You can trust me from now on." The only answer is to BE trustworthy over a protracted period of time. Words are meaningless when trust is eroded. Your partner has to learn to trust you again and that will take some time. The fact is that what was lost in a series of half-truths, lies or deception always takes much longer to repair than it took to cause the damage. That's another reason why this weed is so dangerous.

It is not a "love" issue. It is no good saying, "If you really loved me you would trust me again." That will never remove the weed of mistrust. We all love people we do not trust – like our children for example! We love them but don't always trust their judgement, their replies to our questions or their ability to handle certain tasks. It is, in fact, foolish to trust a person who does not deserve to be trusted. And that is how it is in a relationship where trust has broken down. You can still love your partner but not trust them in certain things. Only as they demonstrate trustworthiness over time will that be recovered.

It is not a "forgiveness" issue. Where the weed of mistrust has taken root the guilty party is often heard to say, "If you had really forgiven me, you would trust me again." But this is also faulty thinking. Forgiveness does not immediately take the relationship back to where it once was. A willingness to forgive is absolutely crucial to the health of any relationship, but just as you can love someone and still not completely trust them, so you can forgive a person and not trust them. And again, it would be folly to do so. The only true remedy for mistrust is to BE trustworthy.

For example, I am short of money and ask you as my trusted friend or partner to lend me some. Because you trust me, you give me a significant sum based on my promise to repay it. Time goes by and you notice I have withdrawn somewhat from the relationship. When you do see me, I never mention the money and you are too embarrassed to raise it. Slowly mistrust takes root. You begin to question whether you will ever see it again. More time goes by. Then eventually I come to my senses and seek your forgiveness for not honouring my promise. Because you are large hearted, you forgive me. Now consider: does that mean you trust me again? And if I asked you for another loan, what would you say? Probably "No" or certainly "not until you prove yourself trustworthy again." I am forgiven but not completely trusted.

Only by making a commitment to the relationship feed of *being trustworthy* can you keep the soil of your relationships healthy and free from the weed of mistrust. Be trustworthy. Tell no white lies. Root out all deception. Have no secret credit cards, liaisons or deals going on that would breach the level of trust appropriate to the nature of the relationship in question. Work hard to keep mistrust at bay by being trustworthy.

The weed: Mistrust

The feed: Being trustworthy

7
Supported

Every now and then I make an attempt to grow tomatoes and it rarely succeeds. So I engage in healthy debate with friends who seem to grow endless supplies of bright red beauties! One asked me, "What are you growing them with?" I misunderstood and talked about the soil and feed I was using. "No," he replied, "I mean what other plants have you put with them?" The question had never crossed my mind! That was my introduction to the fascinating world of complementary planting.

Simply put, some plants benefit from having others planted next to them. So I now understand why people who grow the best tomatoes all seem to like French Marigolds and Tagetes! It is not a coincidence, it's complementary planting. Basically, the scent of the Marigold repels certain insects that are harmful to tomatoes, so it is a form of natural pest control. Very clever.

Gardeners do complementary planting all the time. They will carefully position a tree or shrub to provide shelter from the wind or shade from the sun, or they will position leafy ground-cover to protect the roots of plants which like a cool root – such as Clematis, for example. And so I could go on ... but won't, lest

I bore the non-gardeners reading this! My point being that it really matters what is planted next to what – and it is exactly the same with people. The relationships we grow alongside have a direct affect on our healthy growth, so we need to be doing some conscious "complementary planting" in our relational world.

The fact is that some people are good company and positively enrich our relational world, whilst others are bad company and hinder our relational development. It really matters who you do life with at a whole range of levels.

Now I suspect some of you are pulling back a bit here. Maybe because it all sounds a bit judgemental to be saying a person is "bad company" when, as Christians, we always like to believe the best in people. But stick with me because this is not a black and white exercise. It is not about being judgemental or labelling people inappropriately. It is more about exercising a healthy discretion about who you share which parts of your relational world with.

First, we must never underestimate the impact other people are making on our lives. We do become like the ones we spend the most time with. It is subliminal for much of the time; we gradually adopt their world-view, attitudes and perceptions. Before long we hear ourselves using similar language and expressions as them, our preferences become like theirs and we can even start to look like them. The world is full of examples of this process. Some choose it and aggressively seek to emulate others, but for most it is subliminal and just happens because the process is not controlled. Left unchecked, you are being shaped by every relationship you have – quite a thought!

The Bible makes it clear: bad company *does* corrupt good character (1 Corinthians 15:33) and iron *does* sharpen iron (Proverbs 27:17). If you spend time with an angry person, you *will* become like them (Proverbs 22:24-25). And the same applies to spending time with a gossip, a divisive person or a very positive person.

The company we keep is therefore like the host of other plants in the soil of our relationships. Alongside our primary relationships are myriad others which spring up either like weeds or as deliberate, complementary planting.

Bad company is a weed that if left unchecked will grow and seriously hinder your relationship development with others. Whereas good company is a positive feed, so needs to be encouraged as a form of complementary planting in the garden of your relationships. That is the basic principle here. And as the "Gardener" in this picture, you have to exercise deliberate control over what you allow to grow alongside you.

Now let's get to grips with this more practically because, as mentioned earlier, it is not a black and white exercise. Life is not that simple.

Good can be bad

We need to make an important distinction here: I am dealing with good and bad "company", not good and bad "people". And the fact is that good people can be bad company. That is where this becomes confusing if we are not careful. People who are essentially good, God-loving, friendly, positive and helpful can actually be "bad company" in a specific situation.

Given that we are talking about healthy relationships

here, the impact of this is as follows. You can be in a specific relationship – business, marriage, church, friendship or family – and an essentially good person can have a negative effect on that particular relationship. The good person is bad company. They are like a weed in the soil of that particular relationship that needs to be removed. Whereas others are like feed to that specific relationship; they enrich it, help its development and promote its growth.

I have two friends who each run their own business. Both are good people and have been mutual friends for many years. One is a sole trader working as a tradesman, so all he ever manages is himself and the occasional sub-contractor. The other is the director of a small manufacturing company with a staff of about 25 employees and manages all the challenges that go with that. In the financial crisis that has affected all businesses in recent years, they have supported each other and regularly shared their respective challenges – until recently.

The sole trader is a strong personality with clear opinions that he never hesitates to tell you about. The director, on the other hand, is more compliant and consultative in nature. As such, he tended to absorb the strong opinions of his sole trader friend – and it has cost him. Without realising it, he began to impose certain expectations on his staff that were rooted in what the sole trader thought should happen. You can just hear it: "If I was in charge I would be telling them..." But he wasn't. And more importantly, he had no concept of the challenges faced by his director friend who was trying to believe God and generate enough work for a massive salary bill whilst dealing with complex HR issues that the sole trader had no experience whatsoever in navigating. But he was his friend and a good man. Sadly, the good man became bad company and a weed in the director's wider business relationships. The only answer was to remove the weed and invite the feed of more informed voices into the situation.

I met with them recently and both have learned a lot from the process. The good thing is that they are still friends; they still love trying to thrash each other at golf and they are often seen side-by-side in church with their hands raised in worship. But if asked, the director will tell you his friend is "bad company" when it comes to business development conversations, so he is not included.

This principle is about being discerning not judgmental. Good people can be bad company if we let them too close to a relationship they are ill-equipped to speak into or help develop.

Most of us have best friends who are single when we first marry. They are great buddies and good people who have shared the journey with us. We probably shared everything with them as fellow "singletons".

But they have nothing to say when it comes to growing our new married relationship. They are clueless when it comes to understanding what it is like to live with a wife, navigate the in-laws, balance a budget for two, be considerate of her emotional state, put her first and be a great husband. Thus, good people can become bad company. I have seen too many fledgling marriages rocked by the "bad company" of "best mates" not to mention this.

All relationships have their place. Our challenge is to work hard to ensure the weeds of inappropriate, uninformed or plain bad company do not spring up and choke the healthy development of our primary relationships.

Keep your eyes open

A well-known gardener once said that good gardening is all about observation. He was right. One of the joys of gardening is to meander through your garden each day, to simply take it in and observe what is going on. If a few greenfly or slugs have appeared, you deal with them. You note that the grass needs a cut and plan it in. At the first sign of disease you apply a remedy. You nip off the dead heads daily, tie in fronds that have become too "leggy" and stake new growth that you know will be flattened by the next heavy rain if you don't. And most frequently, you pull up a few weeds. All gardeners can typically be found with a few weeds in their hand because they know the damage they will do if left in the ground. They simply cannot resist pulling them up for the sake of the whole garden.

That is also the attitude we must have to the weed of bad company. Keep your eyes open across all the relationship spheres you enjoy and be a daily gardener. If you spot a relationship suffering because of a person's inappropriate influence, deal with it.

Keep your eyes open for people with specific issues that will choke your relationship if not rooted out. Things like:

- Women who have been wounded in the past by men. If you allow them to pour their hurt out on you as a married woman, it will begin to affect your attitude to your husband.
- Men who despise women because they were once "ripped

off" or rejected by them in one way or another. Don't let their macho-talk and cynicism rub off on you as a married man – it will poison your attitude to your wife.

- Couples who are angry with each other but want to spend time with you as a couple while they snipe away at each other. Don't spend time with people who bring strife and confusion into your marriage however essentially "good" you believe them to be.

- People damaged by a bad previous church experience, who are negative about spiritual leaders, will spread their contagious disease as they speak. Be careful, therefore, how much you listen to.

- The once aspiring but now failed entrepreneur, who is so damaged that he oozes fear and negativity about all forms of business risk and endeavour. Not good company for emerging business leaders.

All these may be essentially good people but are inappropriate, bad company when it comes to keeping specific relationships healthy.

So, keep your eyes open and "weed as you go". Never be afraid to adjust a peripheral relationship for the sake of the health of a primary one: your relationship with God, your marriage, your church, your family, your business or your "friends for life". Only you know what priority each of these may have to you. All I am saying is, guard the most important from the weed of bad company before it takes root and becomes hard to dig out.

Then alongside this, make a deliberate decision to be with people whose words and attitudes draw you closer to each other and the vision you have for your relationship. Find good company; company that is good for the relationship and nourishes its health. Surround yourself with people of similar values, vision and standards. Do things with them, cheer each other on and be there for each other in the tough times. Get busy doing some complementary planting, because by so doing you are proactively feeding your relationships and ensuring their healthy growth.

The weed: Bad company
The feed: Good company

8
Resolved

You join a small group at your church and seem to get on fine with everyone. You sense there is great potential to grow here.

Then one evening Barry makes fun of something you said. Up to then you had been getting on really well with him. But, not wanting to cause a problem, you smile and ignore it.

It happens again.

Then, over the weeks others start to copy Barry and, before long, you feel you are becoming a laughing stock – the fall guy for all the group's jokes. Inwardly you are dying. It hurts, you are angry. You consider speaking up, but don't. It is probably too late to make an issue of it now, you reason to yourself.

So, trapped by your decision to keep quiet, it continues until one evening you announce you are leaving the group because it is not helping you spiritually – and thus the conflict with Barry is avoided. But sadly, none of the real issues ever got tackled and the life-enriching potential of those relationships was never realised.

Let's be honest, none of us like conflict. But in the world of relationships conflict is unavoidable. Our uniqueness guarantees it. We have individual temperaments, personalities, upbringings, experiences, gifts, abilities and passions in life. Those same differences also give colour to life and make relationships interesting. They contribute to the common observation in marriage, for example, that opposites tend to attract. Our mutual diversity enriches all our relationships but is also what creates the potential for conflict. So we do not aspire to never have conflict, rather we aim to manage it when it occurs, putting it to good use in the development of our understanding of each other.

We have a decision to make when things crop up that we disagree about in a relationship. Do we tackle it or do we ignore it? I believe that every time we ignore it, we permit a weed to take root in the relationship which will slowly strangle it.

Because none of us like conflict, there is always a good chance you will ignore it – at least to begin with. But even the smallest ignored conflict leaves a potentially dangerous weed in the ground. Left unchecked, the little things that aggravate you will escalate and become major issues that can lead to separation from the relationship altogether, and all because you chose to ignore the conflict. You chose to turn a blind eye to it and suppress it; you backed off from the confrontation. You have your reasons, I'm sure. Things like fearing the potential pain and tears or rejection you suspect the conflict may expose. But the truth is, you left a weed in the soil of that relationship which grew so large, it severed it.

The process probably escalated through three stages something like this:

1. You had unresolved issues but decided to ignore them.

Rather than getting into it, you **started to tip-toe around certain things**, subjects, names and behaviours. It was like walking on egg-shells. This started to place a strain on the relationship.

2. From this tense place, you try to fix the relationship but still without confronting the root issue. You remain adamant in your choice to ignore the conflict. So you begin to **attack each other rather than the issue**. Instead of saying, for example, "Can we talk about the amount of time you leave me at home" or "the money you spend without consulting me," blanket statements are made like, "You never take me out" and "You waste all our money" or "You never ever help me." Basically, the weed of ignoring conflict is left in tact and the healthy relationship has its life squeezed out of it.

3. Such attacks are never constructive. What started as attacking each other with blanket statements soon escalates further to **attacking the relationship itself**. Things like, "I should have listened to my Mum when she told me not to marry you" or "We probably were never meant to be together." And all because you were too afraid or unwilling to deal with the initial conflict.

If the weed is ignoring conflict, the feed has got to be deciding to resolve issues.

It takes a certain amount of trust and a willingness to make ourselves vulnerable to resolve a relational issue. The knowledge that conflict is coming tests our resolve to deal with anything that will hinder the healthy development of the relationship. It actually makes a statement about how much the relationship means to us. And if it really matters, we will be resolute with this weed and refuse to ignore conflict.

The truth is that relationships are enhanced through conflict. By working through our differences we deepen our understanding and appreciation of each other. It is a totally positive, relationship building exercise if approached properly.

Conflict resolution is a process of finding agreement and unity which strengthens the relationship. It is developmental. It combines the qualities that each person in the relationship brings to it and results in greater synergy and effectiveness.

In a marriage, you fall more deeply in love. In a business you move to a new level of operational effectiveness. In a team you pull together like never before. In a church you submit to one another out of reverence for Christ (Ephesians 5:21) and celebrate one another's contribution to your corporate advance.

Conflict resolution is a life-skill. Learn it and apply it like a feed to the soil of all your relationships. Its elements include:

Recognising your differences

Take account of your differing personalities, approach to life, backgrounds and so on. Acknowledge that they are part of what makes you, you. Affirm one another as unique expressions of God's creative love.

Laughing at yourself

Maintain a sense of humour. Be willing to laugh at yourself and each other as you explore new aspects of the relationship and tackle life's challenges together. Don't take yourself too seriously. Humour relieves the tension. Just never use it to poke fun at your partner in a derogatory way.

Being prepared to change

In the words of Ogden Nash, spoken in a marriage context to husbands, "To keep your marriage brimming with love in the loving cup: When you are wrong, admit it. When you are right, shut up." Have the humility to remember that you could be wrong. The Bibles says, *"A man who refuses to admit his mistakes can never be successful. But if he confesses and forsakes them, he gets another chance"* (Proverbs 28:13 TLB). Willingness to humble ourselves, admit we are wrong and make positive changes for the benefit of our partner and the relationship, is like high grade fertilizer. It feeds the relationship immensely.

Being honest

The deepest form of communication is to be completely honest with each other. This includes expressing your genuine views, heartfelt opinions and real expectations. Be honest about the good and the bad. Only then can the power of true resolution feed the relationship.

Picking your moment

Find the best time to talk about the issue. There may never be an ideal time, but some are better than others. In families, tea time and early evenings are always stressful – so avoid it. Late at night, when you are both tired, may be a bad time for you. Or maybe it is your best time as only then is the house in relative peace. Also, have an awareness of each others body-clock. Do it when you are most alert, relaxed, or mentally up for the hard conversation that's coming.

Listening before you speak

Listen to one another intently. Give space for each to express themselves. Pay attention to more than the words. Listen for what is not said. Watch the other person's body language. As the Bible says, *"Be quick to listen and slow to speak"* (James 1:19). Listen to the attitude, motivation and heart behind the words.

Speaking the truth in love

Then when you do speak, be sure your words are constructive. Avoid accusations, broad generalisations and blanket statements. Make each statement count. Let it add to the resolve and not be about scoring points against each other. As God's word exhorts us, *"speak the truth in love"* (Ephesians 4:15). Be honest, yet loving to the core.

Facing the issue together

Most conflict resolutions require both parties to contribute to the solution. You must therefore face the issue together. It is not your problem, it is *our* problem. Take a step back from the issue together and discuss solutions. Think: Have we isolated the real issue here? Have we both expressed our views honestly? What can we each do to help resolve this? Of our options, which shall we try first? Tackle it together and it will strengthen your relationship.

Re-centring your relationship

Set the issue you are in conflict about in its bigger context. Step back and keep it in proportion. And for Christians, re-centre your relationship as Christ-followers. Recommit to doing things

God's way, which requires mutual respect, being honest, praying for one another and together. The old maxim that says, "The closer a couple individually get to God, the closer they will be to each other" is accurate. What's more, it can be applied to all relationships. Be God-centred in all of them and just watch them thrive.

Ignoring conflict is a weed. It will slowly kill your relationships. So, stop and be willing to have the hard conversations before they become even harder. And I believe you will be sweetly surprised by the feed that enriches your relationships just because you were willing to resolve issues.

Give your partner in your marriage, team, family, business or church a gift – the gift of your willingness to resolve issues. Have a culture that readily says, "Come on, let's resolve this..." and build some healthy relationships.

The weed: Ignoring conflict
The feed: Resolve issues

9
See

We live in a culture that says, "If it feels good, do it!" – but which does not necessarily count the cost of "doing it".

Boy meets girl. They fall in love, get engaged then marry. They vow to stay together "until death separates us". That is a long time. But inevitably they hit difficulties. Now what? Some struggle through, some separate and too many get divorced.

My question to the divorcees is, "Was that ever in your plan?" All would say, "No." So maybe a more fundamental question is, "Was there a plan?" Because all relationships hit tough times and the possibility needs to be fully thought through before the initial commitment is made for the relationship to thrive and survive. What's more, that plan needs to be "life-size" to adequately do the job.

Businessperson meets creative genius. One has the funds, the other the ideas. They join forces. A cutting-edge concept is developed, funded and launched. All looks good. Then they hit problems. The business grows too fast or too slowly. Maybe cash flow issues emerge. Or philosophical differences about business practice, profit sharing or staffing divide the eager entrepreneurs. Matters become insoluble and the promise-filled partnership dissolves into acrimony, separation or even bankruptcy.

I have the same question for these business partners, "Was it in the plan?" Again they will reply, "No." So I am left reflecting that they most probably did not think through a sufficiently robust plan that was "life-size" and able to carry them through difficult times.

Christian visits church for the first time. She feels immediately at home and falls in love with its ministry, ethos and vibe. Feeling empowered by its teaching she decides to relocate to become more involved. Then reality kicks in. This church is not as perfect as she thought and finding her fit is harder work than anticipated. It seems living here is different to being a visitor. Disgruntled, she withdraws to the fringe and soon leaves disillusioned.

Same question: "Was it in her plan?" "Certainly not!" And again I am left wondering whether she actually had a truly thought-through, life-size plan that would steer her though the relational difficulties that accompany every integration into a new church.

Like these people, we are all tempted to enter significant relationships based on a good feeling, a wave of enthusiasm, an emotional impulse or the promise of personal gain. But, like them, it is always doomed to fail unless we have a vision for the relationship and a thought-through, considered plan to act as a frame of reference for when problems occur – because they will.

In the soil of every relationship this little weed of short-sightedness can very quickly take root and must be dug out. It gets in early, that's the problem with this one. It is often rampant before the relationship can become fully established. But, I assure you, it is dangerous and potentially terminal, because it affects the start of the relationship. It gets in the way of a relationship becoming properly established.

So what do we do? We ensure that at the start of every relationship we add into its soil the essential feed of vision. Vision is essential if a relationship is to succeed. Therefore, my question to you is, "Do you have a vision for your relationships?"

I can sense the quizzical look on some readers faces right now. "A vision?" you are thinking, "What on earth is he on about?" "Doesn't he realise that relationships develop, so you cannot have it all planned out in advance?" Yes I do. And I am not suggesting you have every detail nailed down. But I am suggesting that every relationship needs a vision that is large enough to carry its partners through whatever lies ahead. It must be life-size in the sense of thinking through potential outcomes and consequences of the commitment you are making to enter a specific relationship.

Life is constantly changing. It changes us and those we are in relationship with. It throws up all manner of challenges, some foreseeable and others totally unforeseen. But even so, you can have an essential vision that will keep you in tact when difficulties occur. Without a vision, relationships quickly drift apart in a sea of confusion.

The need for vision in a relationship becomes apparent when a problem crops up. At that point we are left asking, "What do we do now?" Without a vision, we have no idea how to respond in the present; no context, no boundaries and no guiding principles. Without a vision, responses and reactions become short-sighted and short-termist. We resort to quick fixes rather than responding from within the framework of our agreed vision.

As the Bible says, *"Where there is no vision, the people perish"* (Proverbs 29:18). One version says, *"...are unrestrained"* (RSV) which gets to the point I am making. Vision constrains you positively. But without it, people in relationships simply *"stumble all over themselves"* (MSG). The vision for the relationship constrains the parties to it – it unites them and galvanizes their responses in accordance with their agreed expectations. Without a vision, we become a shambles.

So, particularly at the start of a relationship, look out for the weed of short-sightedness, because it will make you do rash things. Slow down and deliberately apply a dose of the feed called vision.

Vision develops

The nature of vision is such that you establish it strongly at the start but then have to allow it to develop in line with the progress of your relationships. For example:

• **Getting married?**
Then think: what do we want our marriage to be like? Which other couples inspire us? What will the enduring culture of our family be? Consider all aspects and eventualities. You may, for example, have a vision that includes having children. But it is harder to anticipate when they will arrive, how many you will have, what sex they will be, whether they will be healthy or have complications. And what if you can't have them naturally?

The vision is set: children are in the plan as a non-negotiable, the details will just have to be navigated within that vision as they occur. That is what I mean when I say the vision is set and affirmed, but then has to develop and be reaffirmed at key points on the journey.

I have conducted well over a hundred weddings and none of them set out planning to divorce. The vision always includes staying together forever, 'til death us do part! But that vision gets tested by career development, children, financial limitations, health issues that emerge, wider family pressures, silly things you do, poor choices you make and a host of other things. Again, the vision for the relationship has agreed essential elements, but they will need to be affirmed and developed at key stages on the journey.

So, talk through the hard questions, communicate – which, we remember, is another relationship feed in its own right – and be inspired as you develop a God-centred vision for your marriage. It will be so much stronger for it.

• **Going into business?**
Then talk together about which other businesses you want to be like? What models inspire you? What will your business ethic be? How do you plan to grow, to staff, allocate profits and expand? And what if the market crashes? Be real. Be bold and take considered risks in line with your vision for the partnership. There will be fewer nasty surprises if you do.

• **Making new friends?**
Then sometimes it is good to have a chat with your existing close

friends about where the new one fits. As you navigate life and enter new seasons, keep one step ahead by maintaining a vision for your significant friendships. How will your getting married affect them? If you take that new job, what will happen to them? It is all good feed for the relationship and rescues you from a relationship being ruined by the weed of short-sightedness.

Finally, all I have said about the weed of short-sightedness and the feed of vision has been illustrated from the "front end" of a relationship. And rightly so, I think, because it is particularly important then. Vision is a great "weed suppressant" against short-sightedness. But be warned, the weed can spring up at any time in a relationship and lead to bizarre behaviour.

For example, people leaving a relationship suddenly. One minute they are in church and the next they have gone. The couple who seemed so "together" but now one has moved out. And so on. We have all seen it and wondered, "Why did they quit so suddenly?" Usually we conclude that there must have been things going on we were unaware of. But it's not always the case. Sometimes it is simply that at a new life-stage, season or significant adjustment in a relationship, vision was not developed and the weed of short-sightedness took root. Suddenly the "grass seems greener" with a different partner, a job change, a church move or friendship adjustment, and off they go. Of course, it rarely is when the decision is based on short-term gain. What has been displayed is a fundamental lack of vision for the original relationship.

So, just as I am suggesting you should not start a relationship in a short-sighted way, don't decide to terminate a relationship in a short-sighted way either. It may feel good for a while, but the feeling will not last. Don't rush into divorce: count the cost, the implications on everyone connected to you are massive. Don't rush to dissolve the business partnership: count the cost because it may leave you with debt, the inability to be a director again and a black mark against your reputation. Don't rush to leave the church: count the cost of a potentially hasty decision on your friendships, family, personal spiritual growth and happiness.

Wherever this finds you, I pray that you will guard against the weed of short-sightedness in all your relationships. Root it out! And develop a positive, God-centred vision for your relationships, which will act like a weed-suppressing feed and guarantee future fruitfulness.

The weed: Short-sightedness
The feed: Vision

10
Enjoy

Oh my! This friendship is *so* special. Being married is fantastic. Having children is such fun. Work is invigorating. My small group at church is an amazing growth opportunity. Sunday church is awesome. Serving on this team is so exciting. And so it should be.

Relationships are interesting, engaging, stimulating and fun. That is why we enter them. They promise to invigorate and enrich our lives with their momentum and energy. So we select our relationship partners with care to ensure these positive dynamics are present.

"Come on, let's be friends! This is going to be SO good. Whoopee!"

The problem is that in the fertile soil of these life-enriching relationships, there lies a seed. It is ever present, just waiting for conditions to ripen. Once the excitement has died down a bit, it will start to pop its green shoots through. It waits for the honeymoon period to pass, the initial enthusiasm to fade, the excitement of the launch to become a memory, the fresh start to seem an age ago. Then up it pops and announces itself with the words, "I'm bored!" That seed belongs to the weed called boredom.

Everything in life can become boring, if we let it. And "letting it" is the issue. This relationship choking weed can only take significant hold in our relationships if we allow it.

It works both ways. If previously fun-filled relationships can become boring, then they can become fun again. It is all a matter of attitude and application. There is a process to work with and a set of skills to cultivate here. There is a feed that needs to be regularly applied to our relationship soil, the feed of making it fun.

Let's be honest, we have all become bored in a relationship at one time or another. Marriage can become stale and boring. Family life can disintegrate into a round of monotonously repetitive elements. Church becomes the "same old, same old" pattern. Just boring. Work is tediously repetitive. Flat boring. Before long, you come to regard your town or city as boring, your friends and family as boring and life itself as boring. "Aaaargh! I just need some fun," you cry.

That cry is your first mistake. The cry implies fun comes from others, from outside of you. Fun is out there somewhere, you just need to go and get it – or so you think. The world is full of people sat by tropical pools in exotic places who are bored out of their minds. They spent thousands of pounds to get there to "have some fun", but to their dismay have discovered that, the only problem is they are there too! And they are boring.

The same goes for church. Some people sit in life-giving church services, oblivious to the felt sense of God's amazing presence in the room, the lives that are changing around them and the closeness of Almighty God to them. When asked, they say, "Church is boring", whereas in reality they are the ones who have become boring.

And as for marriage and family ... waking up each day with the same person beside you can become so tedious it's untrue. The same kids, same dog, same route to work, same team, same sandwiches, same TV programmes, same bed. Yawn! Every day is just a predictable round of waking, eating, working, eating again and sleeping. Stop it. You have become boring!

Life is routine. It has monotony built in. We do the same things every single day of our lives. The only thing that changes is our attitude to those things and whether we choose to make them fun or not.

Too many people are waiting for others to make life fun for them, just hoping the more creative types will inject life with a bit of interest for them. How childish.

As parents we manufacture fun for our children. We pull silly faces and put things in front of them to occupy them. But only until they are old enough to begin creating their own entertainment. As they grow, we expect them to develop interests and become interesting as people. We expect them to grow up.

You do not need to *have* fun, you need to *be* fun. Relationships are enriched immensely when we do the routine things in life in a fun way. Attitude is everything. Be the fun you seek and spread it around all your relationships. Because if you don't, the weed of boredom will soon smother the ground with is choking roots and the relationship will slowly stagnate.

We are going to enjoy this!

The Bible makes it clear that our attitude to everyday things should be, "We are going to enjoy this!" Not because of any external stimulus but because we have decided to deliberately enjoy life – however mundane it is. We will make it fun. It will flow from the inside of us, enriching our days. Understanding this Solomon wrote:

*"So I commend the **enjoyment of life**, because there is nothing better for a person under the sun than to eat and drink and **be glad**. Then joy will accompany them in their toil all the days of the life God has given them under the sun."* (Ecclesiastes 8:15)

He later adds to this by saying:

*"Go, eat your food with **gladness**, and drink your wine with a **joyful** heart, for God has already approved what you do. Always be **clothed in white**, and always **anoint your head with oil. Enjoy life** with your wife, whom you love, all the days of this meaningless life that God has given you under the sun ... Whatever your hand finds to do, **do it with all your might**."* (Ecclesiastes 9:7-10)

What a great attitude to life. The key to making life fun is to remember where life comes from – God. Both these verses make the point that we are to enjoy the life "God has given". Gratitude to God makes the Christian relish life, value its potential and enjoy every moment. So, whatever our hands find to do, we "do it with all our might", which includes making it fun.

I have ministered in a number of Third World countries over the years and it never ceases to amaze me how the Christians I meet there can be so happy when they have so little in material terms. It challenges my materialistic, western world-view and reminds me that happiness and fun is never about having things. It is always about our inner attitude, which is shaped by our love for God and our gratitude to him for creating us, saving us, giving us all we have and the ability to enjoy them. God is good and has been good to me, an unworthy object of his love. That amazes me. It makes me happy, content and at peace with myself and the world around me. It liberates me to enjoy every moment of every day – to make it fun.

Fun is injected into your relationships by your attitude. It cannot be bought, borrowed or fabricated. It is something we just have to be. How? By doing ordinary things in a fun way. By laughing at yourself. By being creative, keeping the mood light and relishing every moment. Learn to enjoy every moment of every day. Savour the relationship, thank God for the moments spent together, hug that child of yours and just enjoy the moment. Use your words to encourage your friends and family. Do something crazy. Have your private banter and jokes.

Be yourself. Be interesting. We are all a bit odd if we are honest! We have our quirks, our likes and dislikes. We do things in a certain way, which make the ones we love smile. Don't apologise for loving the things you do; become an expert in them and be interesting with it. It is part of what makes you, you.

But also be interested. Take an interest in the other people in every relationship you have. Draw out of them their uniqueness and celebrate it together. Delight in all that God has made. Laugh, cry, pray, mourn and celebrate together.

Make your motto, "We are going to enjoy this!" and liberally feed the soil of your relationships with a determination to make it fun. If you don't, the weed of boredom will squeeze the life out of every relationship you have and that would be a tragedy.

"A cheerful heart is good medicine" (Proverbs 17:22). It flows from within you, doing you and everyone in your relationships good. So keep dispensing the medicine.

The weed: Boredom
The feed: Make it fun

11
Ardour

It's a warm summer evening. You hoe your soil, dead-head the flowers, neatly stake the ones becoming top-heavy, stand back and feel that simple satisfaction of having tamed nature and created a thing of beauty. Along comes a shower. "It will do the garden good," you think to yourself as you climb the stairs to bed. The next morning the sun is high, the air smells fresh and you stroll out into your garden kingdom – with mug of tea in hand – to savour its delights. And there they are! Weeds. Masses of tiny weeds have emerged overnight in the moist, humid conditions to ruin your masterpiece.

Such is the lot of a gardener when certain conditions prevail. Some weeds pop up fast and are quickly drawn to the attention of the vigilant gardener – much like in our relationships. So, swift action follows and the little pests are easily removed to the compost heap, allowing the plants to grow unhindered. The sooner we clear our relationship soil of the weeds we are exploring in this book, the easier they will be to remove and the better the relationship will be.

But not all weeds are like that. Some, by contrast, grow very slowly – so slowly that you hardly notice them. And when you do, they are very difficult to get out. They make their progress below the surface, spreading their root systems widely and entwining themselves around the roots of healthy plants and sucking the life out of them. I have a weed like that in my front garden and it drives me crazy. When its green shoots emerge I pull it up, but only to find it is attached to a web of roots that seem to run the breadth and depth of the garden! That weed reminds me of a particularly difficult, deep and all pervasive relationship weed we need to be on our guard against: apathy.

Apathy is never present when a relationship starts – it simply cannot thrive where there is passion and excitement about the potential for a new relationship. It tends to appear well after the honeymoon, after two, three or maybe four children have come along in the family. Its foliage will only be seen after your business has been running for quite some time and settled into a good flow or after you have been in your church for a few years. That "foliage" is seen in three tell-tale statements: "I just can't be bothered", "I'm not interested" and "I don't care".

In fact, they may not even be stated in actual words, because their sentiment can ooze from our attitude about a particular relationship we once thought was amazing. It just becomes obvious that we no longer care, are not interested or can't be bothered to expend the energy required to bring change.

You always used to bring your wife a gift home when you travelled away on business, and it was always appreciated, however small or silly. It was the thought that counted. But these days you just can't be bothered.

You always used to listen to the podcast, or get the CD, of the message at church after you'd been away on holiday or business. You didn't want to miss a thing God was saying to you as a bunch of people in a very special relationship. But these days you are just not interested and can miss weeks on end without batting an eyelid because of your disengaged mind-set. "What does it matter what the preacher said?" oozes from your attitude.

When little Amelia first started school, every day you wanted to know what she had been doing, learning about and who she had been playing with. But now she is a teenager and, frankly, you just don't care what she did at school today so never ask. "She's probably not gonna tell me anyway," you reason to yourself. "Teenagers!" And parent and child slowly drift apart on a sea of apathy and lack of interest.

Apathy is defined as the "lack of interest in anything, or the absence of any wish to do anything; the inability to feel normal or passionate human feelings or to respond emotionally". It seems to me that apathy is, therefore, a major relationship killer and a weed we must keep well on top of. To do so we must understand a little about how this insidious weed works.

Apathy feeds apathy

Like all these relationship weeds apathy starts small. But as described earlier, it tends to start its growth under the surface, in the mind and heart of those in the relationship. Something eats away at their mental, emotional and then physical resolve to keep working on the maintenance and development of the relationship.

The thing to understand about apathy is that it feeds on itself. So, once there is a little shoot of it in your relationship soil, it has the potential to spread. That is why we have to be diligent.

It works like this.

The husband who always used to bring a gift home for his wife one day thought to himself. "Why am I doing this? What has she done for me recently anyway? I don't think I will bother – after all, she isn't bothered whether I do or not." His apathetic response was based on the apathy he perceived in his wife. He perceives that she has not done anything for him recently and that she doesn't really care whether he surprises her with a gift or not. Whether this is true or not is another issue, but her "apparent" apathy fed his apathy.

No doubt she will have noticed and thought to herself, "He doesn't think of me when he is away any more. So why do I bother going out of my way to make his favourite meal and trying to make his homecoming special? He can get himself whatever he wants from the freezer!" Now his apathy has fed hers. So the cycle continues and quietly becomes all-pervading. The weed of apathy is strangling the life out of this once passionate, fun-filled, forward-looking marriage.

The preacher casts a vision for the next phase of advance for the church. Excitement is in the air, but even as he is speaking you are thinking to yourself, "Here we go again. More demands to give my time and money. I mean, what has this church ever done for me? I'm gonna make sure I'm away on the Vision Offering day." You have a perception that the church has been apathetic towards you and that makes you apathetic in return. Be warned! Your lack of interest will deepen and your once life-enriching relationship with that spiritual community is in jeopardy, unless you deal with your apathy.

What's more, apathy makes a relationship vulnerable. It not only does its own damage, but also opens the relationship up to the damaging effects of other relationship weeds like silence and mistrust that we have explored earlier in this book. Before long, your relationship soil is choked with a collection of weeds and the relationship breaks down.

So, what is the answer to apathy? One word: passion! Passion is an incredibly strong relationship feed and has the power to eradicate apathy swiftly and completely. We must stoke the fires of passion for each of our relationships deliberately and consistently.

The thing about passion is that it can be aroused. It's there, it just need stirring up and focussing on. Its dying embers just need blowing on and it will burst into flame again. All it takes is a decision, a determined choice, a deep resolve. And that decision is to do the right thing even when we don't feel like it.

Just do it!

Feeling apathetic about church? Can't be bothered to come, serve or give? Then do the right thing, however you feel. Be in church because God says, *"Let's not give up the habit of meeting together"* (Hebrews 10:25). Give because Jesus says, *"It is more blessed to give than receive"* (Acts 20:35). Serve because without your contribution the whole church is robbed of your expression of God's grace. *"Each one should use whatever gift he has received to serve others, faithfully administering God's grace in its various forms"* (1 Peter 4:10).

Get passionate about the big picture, the mission of the church, all you are building together and the lives you are changing. Fan into flame your love for Jesus and his cause. Let zeal for God's House consume you!

It takes effort, focus, and a decision, but if you will make it, that decision will feed your church relationships like miracle-grow!

Feeling apathetic about your marriage? Then revisit the reasons you married in the first place. Rekindle the fires of your love for each other. Make room for intimacy; share what you love about each other. Reminisce about the good times and the bad. Celebrate your successes and remember the hard lessons you have learned together on the journey of life. Laugh out loud, play-fight, dig out the old photos, surprise each other. Communicate, communicate, communicate – enough said! Words of love and passion for the relationship will culminate in love-making as God intended, the deepest expression of love between a man and a woman who have committed their lives to one another.

It is a choice. Do it however you feel! And apathy will become a distant memory, a weed unable to ever get itself established in your relationship again.

Feeling apathetic about your business relationships? Get passionate about the reason you are in business. Have vision meetings with your team, rally the staff, give them incentives, share the victories and pull together in the hard times.

We could go on applying this principle to every relationship we can think of, but I am sure you get my point by now. Apathy is a dangerous relationship weed. It feeds on perceived apathy in others, spreading and killing once vibrant relationships. The only cure is passion – a powerful relationship feed which we must liberally and consistently apply to every relationship, whether we feel like it or not.

Uninterested, don't care, can't be bothered?

Oh yes you can.

Just do it!

The Weed: Apathy

The feed: Passion

12
Negotiate

This is a very important chapter because it deals with a skill required to nourish every kind of relationship. This is an indispensable feed – one without which the relationships you are cultivating will never achieve their full potential. More of that shortly.

First let me introduce you to the relationship weed that brings this important feed to most people's attention: Dogmatism.

To be dogmatic literally means to be "rigid". It is personified in the attitude that says, "I am right and that's that." Or, "It is my way or no way." Dogmatic people tend to have strong opinions. Some like to let you know about them too, while others are more quietly determined to get their way. But whether vocal or quiet, they are opinionated, inflexible and unbending – not the best ingredient for a successful relationship.

You would think that people who demonstrated this tendency would never get into relationships in the first place. After all, a relationship is, in essence, a partnership of people working together. It presupposes cooperation and team work. So why would anyone marry, employ or have on their team a dogmatic person? Yet, they do and it then pops up as a destructive weed in the soil of many a healthy relationship well into their development.

I've come across this a lot in relationship counselling. People just did not see it coming and I have pondered why? My conclusion is that it's because in the early stages of a developing relationship, dogmatism is mistakenly thought to be something far more positive. It can be perceived as strength, as people being sure of what they believe and who they are; it is seen as being clear and these are great attributes in a potential partner.

What's more, because opposites tend to attract in some relationship contexts, the "uncertain" are attracted to the "certain", the "weak" are attracted to the "strong" and the "fragile" to the "secure". But if that strength, security and strong opinions are rigidly upheld by someone who is basically dogmatic, the relationship will soon have problems. When difficulties occur, it will seem like a weed has infested the soil of the relationship, whereas in truth, it was probably there all the time but not recognised for what it was.

The truth is that we all have our personal opinions and tend to believe we know best. Given a choice, we would choose to do things our preferred way and to have others join us in doing so. And that's fair enough at one level. But if we start to insist others do it our way or agree with our opinions, that imposition is dogmatism. A line is crossed and the destructive weed begins to choke the relationship by dominating the soil with its opinion.

Give and take

The only solution to dogmatism is to apply the feed of a fresh commitment to healthy compromise. This is what I alluded to at the start of this chapter. Healthy compromise is a must have ingredient in the soil of every relationship. There is no such thing as a genuine human relationship that does not involve compromise, flexibility, or a bit of give and take. It is a very healthy thing and must be applied with love and care into every relationship you have. Without it, the dogmatists will prevail and strangle the life out of your relationships.

The word "compromise" has had a bad press in Christian circles. It is generally taken to indicate an unhealthy mixture of things or used in relation to a person living below the standards of normal Christian living. To "be compromised" is used of people caught in an "in between" situation, somewhere between right and wrong. But that is only one application of the word and why I am qualifying it with the term "healthy". Unless you are willing to engage in *healthy compromise* you will never learn to grow great relationships. Without some give and take, it is over!

Whenever people come together in any kind of relationship, there has to be a degree of flexibility for it to work. It can never be just on one party's terms. Where it is, and one party is ultra compliant while the other dominates everything, you have a very unhealthy relationship anyway and one which could easily become abusive.

Negotiating the terms of a relationship soon gets you to these issues. When a married couple talk through aspects of their shared life they soon discover where they agree or otherwise. The need for flexibility quickly kicks in and the need for a compromise that enriches the marriage is called for – a healthy compromise. It is the same when entering a business relationship, when children arrive in a family, when joining a new team or making a new friend.

Boundaries

To remain healthy, the compromises you make for the benefit of the relationship as a whole must have boundaries. It is important to know when a particular compromise crosses the line and becomes unhealthy. You must spot when healthy compromise becomes a weed like dogmatism or others we have mentioned in this book, which begins to strangle the relationship.

This is where the need for some of our previously mentioned feeds re-emerges – things like vision and communication. Your vision for the relationship sets the boundaries you agree are appropriate and your communication keeps you all on track. Your vision and good flow of conversation about it help you to isolate what is essential and what is non-essential to the relationship.

For example, in a marriage it is essential that the parties remain faithful to each other, do not contemplate divorce and commit to working through every possible problem they meet with God's help. So no compromise is entertained on these. The boundary is clear. But when it comes to the fraught issue of agreeing the best way to cook scrambled eggs – a non-essential – compromise is very healthy if you want your meal!

As Christians seeking to build our relationships in line with God's word, we have a set of values that are essential to our success and fundamentally non-negotiable. So we do not compromise on these. The Bible informs where the boundaries lie in every relationship. Alongside that we have the indwelling Holy Spirit who promises to *"guide us into truth"* (John 16:13) and helps us establish godly boundaries.

It is not, therefore, a healthy compromise to sit back and permit your partner to take part in ungodly activities like getting drunk, gossiping, cheating the tax man or being dishonest. Neither is it a healthy compromise to allow yourself to be treated like a doormat and end up being abused. Those are unhealthy compromises because they seriously damage the godly basis of the relationship.

A healthy compromise does not leave ungodly behaviours or lifestyles unchallenged – it tackles them head on as potential relationship killers. It is often when such behaviours are confronted that any tendency towards dogmatism in the one who has crossed the boundary will be exposed. If they are intransigent, the relationship is in trouble; the weed has taken root. But if they are humble, teachable and open to correction, the relationship will thrive and grow.

Healthy compromise springs from a healthy heart. God says that from the heart – our inner motivational centre – comes the words we speak (Matthew 12:34) and everything we do (Proverbs 4:23). From a healthy heart that wants the best for the other person, and the relationship as a whole, come great compromises.

- If your heart is saying, "I want you to be happy", you will gladly compromise some of your preferences for the one you love.
- If your heart attitude is that you want to understand the other person more than you want to be understood, a healthy compromise is likely to occur in that quest.
- When you truly respect your partner's individuality and settle

that there are some things about them that simply cannot be changed – it's the way they are made – you will healthily compromise for their sake and the development of the relationship.

• The more you value the other person's strengths, abilities and unique contribution to the relationship in your heart, the more you are likely to be happy with a healthy compromise that ensures those things are never squeezed out by you digging your heels in and becoming dogmatic.

Paul instructed us to *"Submit to one another out of reverence for Christ"* (Ephesians 5:21). That involves respecting how Christ has made the other person, all their individual quirks, strengths and weaknesses and is at the core of every healthy compromise.

Make a daily commitment to healthy compromise for the sake of your marriage, family, business, church, team and other friendships. It is an essential nutrient in the soil of your relationships and will protect you from ever being accused of allowing the weed of dogmatism to take root.

The weed: Dogmatism
The feed: Healthy compromise

13
Importance

Life is busy. I'm a husband, father, grandfather, pastor, teacher, principal, writer, travelling speaker, church builder, reader, thinker, golfer, gardener, walker, occasional chef, dog-walker and sports fan. I sleep sometimes too.

I'm sure you have your equivalent list and, like me, when people say "I know you are busy..." you say something like, "Well, I'd rather be busy than idle!" I have come to the conclusion that everyone is busy – or thinks they are. We inevitably fill our days with doing things. Whether they are productive things, the right things or just random things is another question you have to deal with. But for my purpose here, I am assuming you are busy.

The problem with being busy is that all the activity can blind us to some things that are happening right under our nose. Relationships can begin to fragment, but we are too preoccupied to notice. Friendships become strained or cease developing because we are too busy to invest the time needed to keep them healthy, and we are blissfully unaware. If we carry on regardless with our busy schedule, one day we will inevitably get a wake up call. A friend will leave us, our marriage will hit problems or the church will suddenly feel unfriendly – and all because we were too distracted by our busy life to spot the trend developing.

All relationships need cultivating to remain healthy. Time has to be given to them and space created for them to flourish in. It is an appropriate part of our busyness to do so. But as the things we do in life increase in number and variety, there is a danger we can start to take our primary relationships for granted. Time once given to nurture them is slowly filled with our ever-increasing activity. And the more our relationship-building time gets squeezed out by the busyness of life, a little weed takes root that has the potential to kill the relationship altogether: the weed of *inappropriate busyness*.

It invariably takes hold unnoticed. We simply fail to spot that we have become too busy to communicate properly; too busy to have fun like we used to or too busy to spend quality time together.

As a result, the relationship drifts. The vision and purpose you once had for that relationship is now lost in the fog of your busy life. Eventually disappointment sets in and we conclude that, "This friendship isn't as good as I had hoped", "This church is not enriching my life like I expected", or "This marriage is getting me down." Where once there was hope for the relationship, there is now disappointment and disillusion. As God says, *"Hope deferred makes the heart sick"* (Proverbs 13.12). And you are sick. Or to use our analogy, the relationship is choked by the weed of inappropriate busyness.

When these symptoms are spotted, STOP! Inappropriate busyness is a relationship killer. The soil of your relationship needs immediately treating with a very specific relationship feed. You must *prioritise quality time.*

A National Opinion Poll conducted in 1995 by *Care For The Family* showed that the average father spends less than 5 minutes per day in one-to-one communication with his children. Those same children sit in front of the TV an average of 3 hours per day (quoted in *The Sixty Minute Marriage* by Rob Parsons). Not a good example of prioritising quality time. And how often have you heard the old adage quoted: "No one ever said on their deathbed, 'I wish I had spent more time at the office.'" The implication being that the person had been inappropriately busy and needed to prioritise quality time for their primary relationships.

So let's unpack this a bit more. This relationship feed is a compound of two things that work together: "prioritise" and "quality time". First place the emphasis on the word "prioritise".

Prioritise the right relationships

All relationships have an appropriate space in your world – they are spatial. The skill is to know which relationships fit where and to be willing to adjust the spaces they occupy as you navigate the seasons of life. That means keeping them under review. If you don't, busyness can blind you to the importance of a developing relationship and you will mishandle it – and potentially lose it altogether.

Life also changes relationships. My best friend when I was at school is little more than a casual acquaintance of mine today. And that's fine. But conversely, the casual acquaintance of today may one day become a business partner, mentor in church, or even a spouse. Along the way, the space they occupy changes.

So, we must know which relationships to prioritise today.

It's not my place to tell you what your relational priorities should be, so let me tell you about mine. I should say, this order has not always been the case for me, it is a product of my life so far and reflects a shift I have observed in many people as they age beyond fifty-something. My relational priorities are: God, wife, children and family, church, other friends, work.

This is not a random list, it is carefully thought through and represents the flow of life I believe best keeps me relationally in tact:

- My relationship with **God** informs and directs all other relationships, so it is number one.
- My relationship with Kay, my **wife**, is my first responsibility as a husband and man of God. No other human relationship will ever displace it. From our relational strength flows the ability to raise our family and relate to all other people in life.
- My relationship with my children, grandchildren and immediate **family** follow next. I regard them as my primary stewardship responsibility from God after my wife, so they must come next.
- My relationship with my spiritual family, the **Church**, is next. My love for God, my wife and family feed and inform all I do in church. I believe a healthy church experience and involvement should never be allowed to distort or damage my other primary relationships. That's the life flow for me.
- My relationship with other **friends** comes next, many of whom are also part of the church family and my extended natural family.

- My relationship with the **workplace** and those connected to it comes next. Success at work demands God first, wife and family second, church third and then the rest!

For me this works. But I am hardly typical, I suspect, because in reality I work for the church and all the categories here become a bit mixed up. Maybe that is why I have to be more thought through about relational priorities and which relationships I need to attend to when. It has taken me years to settle this and I regret not settling it sooner. So if I can provoke you to do anything through these pages, think about your relational priorities for the stage of life you are in. Let the flow of God's life inform and direct them and give each of them the time they need.

Which brings me to the second element that makes up the relationship feed I've called "prioritise quality time". Now put the emphasis on the last two words: *quality time*.

Prioritise *quality time*

Time spent with people is not equal in value. There is such a thing as quality time. Think about it: you have to work 8-10 hours per day, but may only get 2 hours with your children on an average work day. Which is most important? The children of course, so the 2 hours spent with them will be of a different quality to the longer time spent at work. It is all about focus and deliberately filling the time with meaningful elements.

- Quality time is about what you do and talk about together. When time is short, you make it count for maximum relationship enrichment.

- Quality time is often spent just enjoying each other's company. It is space created just to be together, for one another, to deepen your intimacy, heart-joining and shared interests.
- Quality time costs you – and that is what makes it special to your partner, friend or colleague.
- Quality time also includes communicating face-to-face. Remember, text messages and conversations using social media are not quality time and never will be. Quality time lets you listen to the other person's real heart cry – while looking them in the eye and seeing the tear well up – something an email will never capture.

Therefore, when life gets so busy that you begin to neglect your relationships – STOP! The weed of inappropriate busyness may well be on the advance, so take out your spiritual garden hoe and dig it out. Then take some time to replenish the soil of your primary relationships with a generous dose of feed: prioritise quality time.

Then, step back and smell the roses. Beautiful.

The weed: Inappropriate busyness
The feed: Prioritise quality time

14
Calm

We all handle our emotions differently. Some wear them cheerfully on their sleeve. The moment you meet them you know instantly how they are. They ooze their emotional state, but at least you know where you stand with them. Others seem to bury them completely. Whether they are in pain, mourning, deliriously happy or have just won the lottery their expression remains the same, their voice never modulates and their body language is unchanging. People like that seem complex, a little distant and hard to reach.

A person's emotional wiring plays a significant part in the relationship building process. At each stage of the developing relationship we want to know how they feel: are they feeling happy, sad, disappointed, excited, cautious or neutral about the relationship? It really matters. It is not surprising then, that managing our emotions plays a major role in the success or failure of any relationship.

In the normal run of things, we gradually begin to understand each other as people and usually come to appreciate the emotional make-up of the other person. It is part of what we like about them; it makes them the unique person they are.

All this is fine and a normal part of healthy relationship development. However, from time to time you may experience a relationship that is poisoned with a weed directly linked to this process of emotional management. It is what I call the weed of emotional outbursts.

It is seen both in the lady who looks like she could burst into tears at any moment and the guy who looks like he could explode with anger at any moment. For some reason there is a volatile emotion permanently near the surface and everyone knows it and has probably felt it. As a consequence, they are now on their guard with them. The last thing anyone wants to do is be the trigger for an outburst!

Over time our lady friend gains the reputation of being emotionally fragile and our gentleman friend becomes known simply as an angry man. Both will struggle to build relationships unless they take control of their volatile emotions.

I realise I have made it sound quite easy to spot this weed, but in reality life is not that straightforward. Many times a relationship has been going for a long time before this tendency becomes apparent. The propensity was always there, but controlled, and now life has forced it to the surface. It is like a weed that appears in the soil of your relationship.

The weed of emotional outbursts has just one cure: a healthy dose of self-control. Exercising self-control over our emotions – especially the volatile ones – is a relationship feed we need to consistently apply. If we stop applying it, the weed will rear its ugly head and wreak all kinds of havoc in our relationship garden.

Every person has the power of self-control. It is always a lie to protest, "I just couldn't control myself" in an attempt to justify the damage caused by your emotional outburst. Yes you can. But if you do not exercise it often enough and teach your emotions to stay in check, the emotions will potentially take you over.

For the Christian, self-control is a fruit of the indwelling Holy Spirit (Galatians 5:22). It is evidence that God lives in you and that you are changing into a person with life-qualities more like those found in Jesus. So we have even fewer grounds to make the excuse that we couldn't control ourselves than an unbeliever.

For those reading this who genuinely struggle to manage their volatile emotions, let me give you some help here. Or, if you are in a relationship with someone who is prone to emotional outbursts, hopefully this will help you to help them. In particular, let's think about managing that most volatile of emotions, anger.

So what can we say to help our angry friend?

1. Anger in itself is not wrong

We all get angry. Even Jesus got angry and the Bible indicates God expresses anger. However, God does not have the irrational, capricious anger seen in people without self-control. God's anger is purposefully directed against those who are against him and his holy will. It is what we would call "righteous anger". That is what was being expressed when Jesus turned the money-changer's tables over and threw them out of the Temple.

Anger can, therefore, be a healthy emotion. It is good to be angry about the sickness that threatens to take your child's life. It motivates you to do something about it. It is good to be angry about injustice, abuse and the exploitation of children and other vulnerable people. Righteous anger drives us to do good, to fix things, start ministries and build churches to rescue souls from destruction.

So, anger in itself is not wrong – it is what we do with it that can make it wrong.

2. Understand your anger

We all need to understand how our anger works. Some people explode, others implode. The "exploders" lash out verbally and physically – the Incredible Hulk comes to mind! That is the kind of explosion we fear and do our best to not trigger when we sense it is near the surface in our friend. The "imploders" generally clam up and push the anger deep within themselves, but do not deal with it, so it simmers. They boil inwardly, which is what we, their friends, pick up on and tiptoe nervously around. Who knows, one day it may just all come rushing out in a torrent of hatred and abuse. In the meantime they will most likely become ill with ulcers and stress.

Both lead to personal and relational destruction. Such outbursts of anger damage trust, break lines of communication and violate relationship covenants. The angry person may attempt to exercise control over others through emotional blackmail in a vain effort to hide their problem. But it will not succeed. The relationship will be destroyed unless they take control of their anger.

The beginning of taking that control involves understanding how you tick. Get to know yourself. What sets you off? What are the triggers? Where did they come from and how can they be removed? This is the beginning of learning to control your anger.

3. In your anger do not sin

The Bible says, *"In your anger do not sin"* (Ephesians 4:26). It is a clear command. Within it is the thought that it is OK to be angry about some things, but when you are, don't let the anger make you sin. Don't let it develop. Instead, exercise self-control over it.

I have four children and know what it feels like to be angry with them. Their stubbornness, naughtiness and sheer disobedience has made me angry over the years. That was a good thing. It stirred me to discipline them, help them set boundaries and learn the difference between right and wrong. But if it tipped over into abusing them, being violent with them or exasperating them disproportionately, I would have been be sinning.

Husbands and wives sometimes fall out. They become rightly angry about issues that hinder their relationship development and threaten their togetherness or family unity. All good stuff as long as self-control is exercised. Have the hard conversations, repent, change, forgive and be careful with your choice of words even though you are fuming! But if it becomes a slanging match with threats of withdrawing sex, money or other favours, it has crossed a line and become sin.

An emotionally well-adjusted friend of mine was falsely accused of misappropriating funds at work. He was angry; so angry I thought he would burst! However, that anger became fuel for the appeal process that followed. He built a case, ferreted out the real culprits and registered it, all in strict accordance with company rules. Along the way, however, he was lobbied by a number of other disgruntled employees who urged him to start a campaign to topple the management. We talked about it one day and realised that to do so was inappropriate. It would be getting into someone else's fight and actually become sin for him.

John Ruskin famously said, "He that would be angry and sin not, must not be angry with anything but sin." Wise words indeed.

4. Don't let anger linger

A big step towards the successful self-control of anger is to deal with it quickly. In fact, the very next statement after the Bible commands, *"In your anger do not sin"* says, *"And do not let the sun go down while you are still angry"* (Ephesians 4:26).

What great advice. Make it a policy that when you have an argument and end up feeling angry – even if it involves an outburst – not to let it linger to the next day if at all possible. Don't sleep on it – you'll simply get an ulcer and your mind will stew on it all night long, reinforcing your angry state. Equally, make sure you don't give them the silent treatment for days on end. That is just internalised anger waiting to be vented.

Taking responsibility and controlling your anger quickly is a sure sign of progress on the road to successful anger management. Remember, you can do it. That is why God can confidently command you to *"Get rid of all bitterness, anger and rage"* (Ephesians 4:31).

5. Avoid angry people

As the English proverb says, "birds of a feather flock together", so there is a good chance that an angry person will be attracted to other angry people. That could be a recipe for disaster because anger is an emotion that gets "stirred up" by other people and certain triggers.

The Bible wisely recommends, *"Do not make friends with a hot-tempered man, do not associate with one easily angered, or you may learn his ways and get yourself ensnared"* (Proverbs 22:24). As we have discussed elsewhere, we do become like those we spend time with, so avoid angry people – especially if you have an anger issue yourself.

6. Slow down

So, you are beginning to identify the things that trigger your anger, growing in understanding about how your anger works, determining not to let it linger and avoiding people who may stir it up again. One final thing to add is to generally slow down and, in particular, be slow to speak.

Much of the problem with emotional outbursts is that they are hastily delivered and then later regretted. It is the classic behaviour of a child having a tantrum. No wonder James advised the Christians he was teaching to, *"Be quick to listen, slow to speak and slow to become angry, for man's anger does not bring about the righteous life that God desires"* (James 1:19-20). This indicates we can slow down the speed at which we become angry by listening better and speaking less.

People who fly into a rage always make a bad landing. So develop personal strategies to slow your anger down. Simple things, like counting to ten before responding to certain things. Or leaving the conversation politely and getting some head-space to think and calm down. Or actually saying to your friend, "This is making me angry so please can we change the subject?"

Or calling on Christ to help you handle the emotion you feel building up inside you – after all, the Holy Spirit is within us and his fruit is self-control. You can do this!

7. Deliberately love people

It is hard to genuinely love people and be angry with them at the same time. It is even harder to pray for them and feel animosity towards them at the same time. So, just as Jesus made a deliberate choice to love us when we were unlovable sinners, do the same for those in your world who contribute to stirring up your anger or who have suffered because of it.

The Bible says, *"Love is patient, love is kind ... it is not easily angered, it keeps no record of wrongs"* (1 Corinthians 13:4). Make loving people an act of your will; enlarge your heart for people, be kind, generous and encouraging. Before long, you will feel another emotion that will forever negate your anger – love itself.

You can do this. You have the self-control required. All you have to do is believe it and, with God's help and your supportive friends, you will soon rid your relationship soil of the weed called emotional outbursts.

The weed: Emotional outbursts
The feed: Self-control

15
Respect

Even the best of friendships can dissolve into a fruitless stalemate when strong disagreement takes hold. Unless someone gives ground, it could actually become terminal – or at best the nature of the relationship be forever changed. But usually someone has the sense to back down for the sake of the relationship and the road to the healthy compromise we discussed earlier is embarked on.

I have been involved in relationship conflict resolution for longer than I care to remember and it has left me with an absolute conviction that with God's help, all issues can be resolved if the parties involved want it enough. But sometimes I have found myself fighting for reconciliation harder than the people involved! That's a sure sign I need to back off.

On one occasion I sat with a married couple who were teetering on the verge of separation. Based on what I knew in advance, I reasoned to myself that there was nothing to stop them working it through except their willingness to work on the process together. So I let them speak and steered the exchanges towards my hoped-for reconciliation. I was soon dismayed. Every single situation one described, the other described differently. And not just a little bit differently – completely differently.

It was so bizarre that I had to stop them and say, "One of you is obviously lying." It was that blatant. They were like boxers in the ring throwing punches at each other, both equally determined not to back down, show any sign of weakness, admit any wrongdoing or accept they needed to change. I was so frustrated I refused to see them again until they each agreed to be honest, because one or both clearly weren't being so.

I remember walking away from that encounter disturbed. I threw up a prayer to God for wisdom and he dropped this verse into my mind: *"Where there is strife, there is pride, but wisdom is found in those who take advice"* (Proverbs 13:10). That was it: basically they were both being proud and their pride was keeping the strife alive. Neither had the wisdom to humble themselves and take advice. So how could I ever hope to help until they changed that attitude? I had rightly withdrawn. I felt at peace with my decision.

Pride is a nasty relationship weed – one of the more obvious ones – so I don't need to go on at length about it. The destructive power of pride in a relationship is there for us all to see. And we can all quote the scripture that says, *"pride comes before a fall"* (Proverbs 16:10).

Equally, its remedy is well known: humility. Humility is a vital relationship feed and will be found in all good quality relationship soils. So cultivating humility is a great nutrient for your relationships.

Some weeds in the garden are large and obvious. Maybe pride is like that for the most part. But, like all the other relationship weeds we have explored, this too starts small.

Pride is rooted in a fundamental belief that you are right. Your opinion is the correct one. Your way of doing a certain thing, interpreting a Bible passage, your view of the opposite sex, your attitude to money, God, church or the government is right. As such, it will be defended by you should it be opposed.

Before it became such an entrenched belief – a life-shaping conviction to be fought for – the idea first came from somewhere. It started small, was entertained by you and eventually believed because it pleased you, affirmed your attitude to life, lifestyle choices and world-view. The question is why? Why did you develop such a strong world-view and now defend it at all costs? What does holding that strong view do for you? And what is it covering up?

The danger with pride is that it makes us like God – the ultimate arbiter of what is correct in a given situation – and eventually puts us against God because we believe we know better. That is a dangerous place to get to and explains why God is so opposed to the proud (Proverbs 8:13; 16:5).

The proud decline to get help because they do not accept they need it. They also stop other people in close relationships with them from getting help too – because they are all the help that person needs. Again, I ask why?

So often this springs from a basic insecurity in the proud person and their proud, boastful statements are just a wall of protection to keep people away from seeing their inner fragility and confusion. Pride "comes before a fall" because once the pride is exposed, there is nothing of substance to keep the person from collapsing.

Pride is always a cover for something. It could be for insecurity, poor behaviour, the fear of rejection, or the fear of their inadequacy and lack of knowledge being known by others. As such, it smothers a relationship with its weed-like root system, sucking the life out of the relationship soil and dominating the garden.

By contrast, the wonderful thing about humility is that it springs from a courageous heart. It comes from a person who is teachable and wants to find help when they are confused or in trouble. They are open to correction, willing to learn and keen to take advice. But best of all, they are malleable and willing to make changes in the light of the truth they come to know. Thus, the relationship soil is enriched by humility. It can breathe, receive new stimulus and nutrients, be turned over and worked upon to produce a very fertile soil. And that is the kind of relationship soil we all desire.

- Humility flows from an open heart, but pride keeps a heart locked up.
- Humility releases you to get help, but pride stops you from doing so, holding you to itself in a controlling manner.
- Humility seeks help when it is confused, but pride covers its confusion with confident statements of knowing the answer, even though it doesn't.
- Humility is pure, but pride is twisted and depraved.
- Humility shows wisdom, but pride shows folly.
- Humility changes for the better, but pride is intransigent, stubborn and unyielding.
- Humility comes from heaven, but pride from hell.

So be on guard against all forms of pride and keep your relationships fed with humility.

A final thought: Pride is usually presented to us as "wisdom". It is to be believed and acted upon as the best way to proceed. But the Bible makes it clear there are just two kinds of wisdom available to mankind. One flows from heaven, the other from this world. The question becomes, which kind of "wisdom" do you want to spread on the soil of your relationships? Read what God says and decide:

"Who is wise and understanding among you? Let them show it by their good life, by deeds done in the humility that comes from wisdom.

But if you harbour bitter envy and selfish ambition in your hearts, do not boast about it or deny the truth. Such 'wisdom' does not come down from heaven but is earthly, unspiritual, demonic. For where you have envy and selfish ambition, there you find disorder and every evil practice.

But the wisdom that comes from heaven is first of all pure; then peace-loving, considerate, submissive, full of mercy and good fruit, impartial and sincere." (James 3:13-17)

No contest!

The weed: Pride
The feed: Humility

16
Empower

At some point, every relationship gets tested. Marriages and families come under pressure, businesses go through slow periods, churches make changes that not everyone likes, and the best of friends can have serious disagreements. Only then is the loyalty, trustworthiness and integrity of the parties truly tested.

Relationships that have ridden a storm together are always far stronger than ones that have been plain sailing. One of the things exposed by a storm are our priorities. It tends to show up just what we think is important about the relationship and why we are in it. And sometimes the storm serves to expose that we are using the relationship for our own selfish ends. Events conspire in such a way that one person feels the need to take control of the other to ensure their interests are protected. And thus the seeds of a relationship weed are sown: the weed of controlling behaviour.

To begin with, exercising control over another person or people in the relationship is often seen as a positive thing. It is someone bringing leadership and direction – much-needed elements. And compliant people are easily swept along by the strength of character of another. But where the controlling behaviour is wrongly motivated, it is the start of a very serious problem.

Controlling behaviour in a relationship can have many reasons behind it. But the reasons all have one thing in common – the self-protection of the controlling person. For one reason or another they do not want the relationship to change, which means controlling the other people in it to ensure they get what they want. This weed can therefore be introduced into the soil of your relationship by any factor that threatens the position of the controlling person. Common reasons for its appearance are:

Jealousy. The controlling person dislikes the fact that their friend, or partner, has more fun with people other than them, has more intellectually stimulating conversations with people other than them, or seems to just enjoy someone else's company a bit too much – in their opinion. So they start doing things to control the relationship, thus protecting themselves from losing the relationship. It is all about them.

Material loss. The controlling person relies on the income provided by their partner. Fear of losing that standard of living or lifestyle makes them control the person inappropriately. Or it could be physical support that is received from a carer, practical help gained from a physically stronger person or the promise of a bequest from a rich relative. To lose the person would be to suffer material inconvenience and loss. So they exert controlling behaviour over the person to keep them close. It is all about them.

Insecurity. The controlling person is emotionally dependant on their friend and reasons that they could not live without them. So they won't. To ensure the outcome they want, they work hard to control their friend, thus protecting him or herself from the pain of ever losing the relationship or the possibility of rejection. It is all about them.

Reputation. Some people are very concerned about what others think of them. Their reputation is everything to them. They need to be perceived to be "together", Mr or Mrs Perfect. That perceived perfection is threatened if a relationship becomes dysfunctional. What would the neighbours say? The shame of it! So, control is exercised over others in the relationship to ensure their reputation is kept in tact and the public humiliation of ever having a broken relationship is avoided. In reality, it is all about the controlling persons reputation. It is all about them.

These, and other drivers, can cause a person to exert controlling behaviour in a relationship. Whatever the reason behind the behaviour, it is always selfishly driven for their self-protection at the expense of others in the relationship. And those weeds will strangle the relationship over time and make it unfruitful.

The controlling behaviour itself can look like many things. Here are a few examples from my experience:

Control through **threats**. The controlling person issues threats – sometimes very nicely so as to hide their real nature. They may threaten to withdraw things like sex, money, time with the children, leisure time or other pleasures the other person rightly relies on them for. Or, in extreme cases, they may threaten to hurt the other person if they do not do as they wish.

Control through **blackmail**. People close to you know

your secrets. You have opened your heart and made yourself vulnerable. The controlling person then uses this information to blackmail you. The say they will reveal your secrets. They threaten to "tell your boss" about your true background; they will "tell the police" about a situation in your past, or simply "tell your family" what you really think about them. It can take many forms, but is essentially manipulation through emotional blackmail.

Control through **beliefs.** We all have a belief system and try to live by it. For most reading this book, it will be the Christian faith. Knowing this, a controlling person can use our belief system against us. If they are persuasive, good at quoting the Bible and claim to have the backing of the pastor, they can control weaker, less well-informed people. "It is the will of God for you to serve me," one unemployed man assured his hard working wife while he sat at home all day doing nothing. Another physically abusive husband claimed, "God hates divorce so you can never leave me and go to heaven." I have also seen adult children appallingly controlled by their parents using this tactic for fear of losing them: "Children obey your parents" is quoted as manipulation not to leave home, the area, or withdraw financial support. It is good to have a belief system but never let it be used against you.

Control through **material things.** Some controlling people literally buy their friends and partners. They lavish so much stuff on them that they reason, "They will never leave me now."

Control through **moodiness.** Controlling people will use all manner of emotional and psychological methods to get their way. Their mood pervades the home, business or small group. It is their way or no way. And by projecting an emotion, saying certain things or just having certain body language, they control things. It can range from talking excessively so no other opinion is voiced, through to complete silence for long periods. Tantrums, looking glum, staring coldly at people and being hyper all feature in the repertoire of a person controlling a relationship through their moodiness.

So that is the weed of controlling behaviour. How, then, can we protect against it ever being sown in the soil of our relationships? By adding the relationship feed of being releasing.

To be a releasing person is to always do what is best for the other person. Even though they are our best friend, we release them to be enriched by other friendships too. Husbands release their wives to do the girly things that keep them feminine, and wives release their husbands to get their fix of sport. Families release their loved ones to pursue career opportunities at the other side of the world and churches send out their best people with their blessing to serve God in other contexts.

This large-hearted, people-empowering attitude is a tonic for all relationships. It has the best interest of our friends and partners at its core. It wants them to succeed, to be the best they can be and for them to be truly happy in life. Other-mindedness is wonderful in a relationship. It is a reflection of God's heart for relationships and what he modelled in laying down his life so we could be his friends and family.

The beauty of being releasing in your relationships is that this attitude acts like glue. When you are releasing, unselfish and other-minded, your friends will love you more and stick with you. But the controlling person has a problem, because what they are selfishly trying to cling onto by controlling behaviour, they will lose. It is an absolute certainly unless they change.

God says this about our willingness to release what is of value to us: *"One person gives freely, yet gains even more; another withholds unduly, but comes to poverty"* (Proverbs 11:24). This principle applies to relationships, those precious friends we love to do life with. If we will give them freely – be releasing – we will gain more. But if we cling to them in a controlling manner, we will end up in relational poverty. So, keep the weed of controlling behaviour well away from the soil of your healthy relationships by enriching it with a releasing attitude. Be other-minded, not selfish, and relationships will thrive.

The weed: Controlling behaviour
The feed: Releasing

17
Wisdom

As we established at the start of this book, we must be like good soil, which hears the "message of the kingdom" and allows God's wisdom to sink deep into its fertile soil, the result of which will be fruitful relationships.

This final weed is no exception. In fact, it is something of a "catch-all" because many of the other weeds we have identified so far could also be described as being this one too. But then, that's what weeds are like! Many of them look remarkably similar to each other at first glance, which is why we have to become relationship gardening experts.

Have you ever made a bad choice? By "bad choice" I mean choosing to do something that has had a negative effect on a particular relationship. And of course the answer is "Yes". We all have. It's part of life. We learn how to make great choices by trial and error, so making a few bad ones along the way is normal.

However, those bad choices sometimes become far more than just a passing mistake we can quickly remedy, learn the lesson and move on from. A bad choice can become a nasty, lingering weed in a relationship if it is not dealt with.

Relationships are always put under strain when one party makes what proves to be a bad choice. How often have you looked back and thought to yourself, "That was a bad call." It may have been a choice to spend money on something you now realize was a waste of money – and your partner is none too pleased. We have all said things and later regretted the way we said it – a bad choice of words. A hasty move is often regretted later and seen as a bad choice. We come to a realization that spending time with certain people was a bad choice, leaving a job when we did was a bad choice, or even taking the new one.

Our greatest power is the power to choose. And when we are in close relationships with other people, every choice we make affects someone else. So learning to exercise that power correctly, by choosing things that bless, enrich and strengthen our relationships is the best possible knowledge to acquire. The truth is that we do not have to engage in conversations that are destructive, or live in a cycle of losing our temper and seeking forgiveness. We do not have to live perpetually "walking on eggshells" because relationships are so fragile. We do not have to drink that alcohol, watch that porn, hit that person, use foul language, tell that lie or walk away from that relationship ... It is always a choice.

"All-round" feed

The weed of bad choices must be kept at bay from the soil of our relationships by having a commitment to acquiring wisdom. The best possible, all-round, relationship feed is to get wisdom.

God says, *"Get wisdom, get understanding; do not forget my words or swerve from them. Do not forsake wisdom, and she will protect you; love her, and she will watch over you. Wisdom is supreme; therefore get wisdom. Though it cost all you have, get understanding"* (Proverbs 4:4-7).

That says it all. Great relationship choices are made as we commit to a life of gaining wisdom.

In my pursuit of gardening excellence I like to find out what each plant in my garden needs to thrive. Does it like sun or shade, moist or well-drained soil, to be pruned in spring or autumn? Do I use ericaceous compost or a less acidic one? Getting technical now! – but relationship gardening is no less complicated. In the pursuit of relationship gardening excellence I must work equally hard to gain the required wisdom, otherwise I will keep making the same bad choices and my "plants" – my relationships – will suffer.

Relationship wisdom is available. It is not the exclusive province of pastors and relationship counsellors – it is available for all if they will take the time to seek it out. The Bible makes it clear that, *"If any of you lack wisdom, he should ask God who gives generously to all without finding fault, and it will be given to him"* (James 1:5). So it is there. However, it has to be searched for. By "searched for" I don't mean it is hard to understand, just that it takes time and effort to search it out. But most of it is simple, uncomplicated and plain common sense once you have understood it.

Wisdom has a way of giving itself to the true searcher – the one desperate enough to buy the relationship book, ask for advice, attend the relationship seminar, be teachable and demonstrate the heart of one who is out to "get wisdom". It was Jesus who said, *"Ask and keep on asking, knock and keep on knocking, seek and keep on seeking"* (Matthew 7:7 Amplified). True seekers are the ones who gain the most wisdom in life. In fact, it is the journey of seeking wisdom itself, the effort of acquiring it and the cost a person is willing to pay for it that shapes them to be the wise people they are. Relationship wisdom doesn't just drop into your lap, it has to be searched for. But deciding to seek it is one of the best choices you will ever make in life.

Get yourself some relationship books. Have a look at the reference list at the back of this one and there you will find a selection of ones I have found helpful. Go on a relationship development course – it may well save your marriage or business. I find that many people are too proud to admit they need help with their relationships, so going to a marriage enrichment seminar that might imply they have a problem is never an option. But in reality it is just another bad choice!

Talk to people who are older, wiser and further down life's relationship road. Pick their brains, learn from their experience and make it your mission in life to not repeat the relationship mistakes you observe in others.

Read your Bible. In it you will find how God created us to conduct all and every kind of relationship. Whether you are a husband, wife, best friend, neighbour, employer, employee, mother, father or child – it is all in there.

It takes wisdom to build, to grow, to navigate, to cultivate, to develop and to manage your relationships. God's word – the message of the kingdom – says, *"By wisdom a house is built, and through understanding it is established"* (Proverbs 24:3). So go get yourself some. It is the best choice you can make.

You will discover that wise words build a great relationship, but rash, foolish words will tear it down.

By gaining wisdom you can break the generational patterns that may be shaping your poor choices. You do not have to be a repeat of the dysfunctional family you grew up in or the broken society around you.

Wisdom will also stop you doing what's sometimes in your head – those hasty decisions remain unmade, the cruel words are set aside, the tantrum is never expressed and the anger quashed before it has time to boil over.

Wisdom sets the pace for your relationships, determines their culture and shapes their values. Wisdom takes control and designs a relationship rather than allowing it to drift into a dysfunctional default setting.

Wisdom is not emotionally driven or reactionary, but finds its centre in God and his pattern for healthy relationships.

So, if you are reading this knowing your relationships are suffering because of a bad choice you made, get wisdom. Find out how to resolve it once and for all and do it for the sake of everyone in the relationship.

And, if you are reading this knowing your partner, or someone in your relationship matrix, has made a bad choice that you are a victim of, get wisdom. Be part of the answer. Don't put your life on hold, stay trapped or sit there feeling helpless. You too have the power to make bad choices or to seek wisdom that will restore and enrich the relationship.

Made a bad choice? Get wisdom.

The weed: Bad choices
The feed: Get wisdom

18
Get Your Hands Dirty

I love strolling around a well-tended show garden on a summer's day. The carefully nurtured plants are in their prime, bursting with life and fragrance. Skilful planting has ensured that each is in its best setting and alongside complementary blooms, making the whole display a feast of colour and interest. Every now and again I spot a new species which enchants me, but most of the time I am simply taking pleasure in the glorious show of well-known plants creatively grown together. And like all aspiring domestic gardeners, I stand back and think, "I wish my borders were as good as these."

But they never are. Partly because my garden has different soil, growing conditions and microclimate, whereas theirs always seems to be somehow "ideal". And more crucially, I am just not as dedicated a gardener as the staff who look after the show-gardens.

Relationship gardening is exactly the same. We go places and meet people who seem to have it all together. Their relationships are like a show garden. From them we learn the occasional new thing, but most of the time we just admire their ability to grow the same thing as we are growing – a family, marriage, business, church or friendship group. But they seem to be doing it more effectively than we are.

The reasons are equally similar. They are growing relationships in a way that best suits the "relationship soil" of their unique personalities and the "growing conditions" of their specific circumstances, life-stage or environment. But again, more crucially, they are dedicated "relationship gardeners" and pay regular, close attention to nurturing their relationships.

That is the challenge as we draw our thoughts to a close. How dedicated a relationship gardener are you prepared to be?

Real relationship gardeners

One thing always impresses me about a good show garden: its lack of weeds. Where soil is visible, the carefully clipped lawns frame the dark earth, which in turn blends into the formal planting. Not a weed to be seen anywhere!

This is not an accident. Well before the visitors entered the show garden a team of gardeners were up bright and early, pulling up any little weeds that had appeared overnight to keep the exposed soil healthy. But as the summer goes on, the mass of weeds are kept out simply by the abundance of the planting itself. The good plants fill the soil, leaving no room for weeds to take root or thrive.

Relationships are identical to this. They need regular attention to keep all the weeds we have identified in this book at bay. But more importantly, the relationship needs to thrive and become so well established that it leaves no room in your relationship soil for weeds to flourish. Feed your relationships, cause them to flourish and let the range of your relationships totally fill the relationship soil you have available.

Garden Centres have made gardening easy for us. These days we can even buy a ready-made garden in a pot. We turn up, browse the stock, make a purchase and stand the pot on our patio or pop the plants into our borders. For a season we have colour and the appearance of gardening excellence – then autumn comes and it all ends up on the compost heap or in the bin. So off we go to the Garden Centre again to see what they have for the winter and come back with winter pansies, ivy and hardy evergreens. By spring we are desperate for colour again, so go and buy a pot of daffodils or hyacinths to see us through until the last frost passes and we can get those bedding plants in again. Round and round we go. This is not real gardening.

Real gardening sows the seed in well-prepared soil, tends the young shoots until they are hardy enough to be planted out and feeds them appropriately. Attention is paid to the plant regularly. It is fed, watered, pest-controlled, pruned, dead-headed, cut back as required and tended for maximum fruitfulness. Real gardening requires constant observation and intervention; it means getting your hands dirty!

A real gardener not only gets their hands dirty, they know their plants. They know some are with them for the long haul – the perennials that come back year after year. Whereas others are annuals, adding colour and fragrance for just one season and then they are gone – living on only in the photo album.

Real relationship gardeners do the same. They understand the need to get their hands dirty and to get their spiritual and relational garden tools out regularly, so they can have a fruitful "garden". They know which relationships are perennial and which are annual. Marriage is for life – a perennial. Whereas some friends will enter our lives for just a short time and move on – annuals that live on in our photo albums. The skill is in *relationship identification* and ensuring you nurture each one accordingly.

Writing this book has been driven by a burden – a deep desire from God – to help people have fantastic relationships. That is what God wants you to experience and enjoy. He does not want you to lurch from one relationship dysfunction to another, he wants you to become a skilful relationship gardener – someone who is nurturing all their primary relationships with care and attention to achieve maximum fruitfulness. That is never about crisis intervention, but always to do with the daily disciplines of relationship management. But should a relationship ever become so damaged that crisis intervention is needed, get it fast! Then once mended, develop the daily disciplines of nurturing and feeding it like a real relationship gardener.

Watch – dig – feed

I leave you with three practical things to do. These are the attitudes and actions of the skilled relationship gardener you aspire to be.

1. Watch. Relationship development is all about observation, being vigilant, keeping watch. As people we are constantly changing, so we must respect and allow for that in each other. In particular, keep watch for the early signs of disconnection. Rarely do relationships break suddenly. When they do, there was always a process we simply missed. There can be lots of reasons why we missed it, of course, but never let it be because we were not observant enough.

I have noticed that people generally disconnect from a relationship in one of two ways: either deliberately or accidentally.

Deliberate disconnection is where one party makes a conscious choice to pull back from the relationship. It may be in favour of what they believe is a better one for them, or because they feel abused or unwanted. Reasons abound. But for reasons best known to them the person uncouples from the church, business, family or friendship. This is a deliberate, purposeful choice motivated by things only they can articulate.

Accidental disconnection, on the other hand, is where a person perceives they are now "outside the group" but do not really understand why. They have not deliberately withdrawn, but it seems they have. They suddenly feel disconnected from church, the family or the team and it is not a good feeling. "How did this happen?" They are left pondering.

Accidental disconnection often happens because of unforeseen things in life. Life just happens! People get sick or die, jobs are lost, friends relocate, church goes through a leadership change. Life bumps into us. It is like a trailer attached to a vehicle going over a bump in the road – sometimes they disconnect and the driver is oblivious to the fact. Similarly, you went through a hard time, a bump in the road of life, and you never noticed a relationship had become disconnected as a result.

That is why you must keep watch. It prevents unwanted disconnection caused by the bumps of life, as well as ill-advised deliberate disconnections. However it happened, once spotted, you must deal with your disconnect. This is a personal process that involves three steps:

a. Admit it

Nothing can be resolved when a relationship disconnects without an honest admission of the problem. So, admit it!

Awareness of our disconnection is frequently reached in a moment with God. When we quieten the voices of others and our own protestations, God can clarify what is happening for us. Remember the disciple Thomas? He was disconnected from the group of disciples for a week because he had simply not been there when Jesus appeared. Whatever the group said, he was resolved not to believe them. His attitude was closed, heart was hard and ears were deaf. Until, that is, Jesus had a face-to-face with him (see John 20:27-28). His moment with Jesus caused him to admit his doubt and disconnection.

We see the same in Peter who denied Jesus. He was deaf to Jesus' warnings because of his self-confidence and bravado, but still denied him three times. When it happened we read, *"The Lord turned and looked straight at Peter. Then Peter remembered the word the Lord had spoken to him: 'Before the rooster crows today, you will disown me three times.' And he went outside and wept bitterly"* (Luke 22:61-62). It took a face-to-face with Jesus for him to admit he had disconnected. The realisation broke Peter because he now felt what Jesus felt about his disconnect, and so must we.

Working pastorally with God's people for over 30 years has taught me that it does not matter how many times I tell you that you are disconnected, you will not hear it until you look into the face of Jesus! That is why you need to be in church, engaged in the worship, listening to God's word and have a close personal walk with him.

b. Act on it

Action must follow the admission of being disconnected or you will end up living in turmoil. So, take active steps to reconnect as appropriate.

Life goes on, even when we are disconnected. It's just not a very nice life. So the quicker we act the better. After Peter had denied Jesus and subsequently admitted to himself his disconnect from his Lord and the group of disciples, life went on. He was still at the tomb when Jesus was raised from the dead, as well as when Jesus appeared to the disciples on two occasions. He must have been wrestling with what "getting on with life" now looked like. But he was doing his best to stay close to Jesus and the group of disciples – but I am not sure he always felt like doing it.

This is the painful part: you may well have to do things you do not feel like doing. To reconnect you will have to reach out to people, be in church, love your wife or husband, get advice or counsel, read your Bible, change your lifestyle or friends. You just have to do what is needed to repair the disconnection, however you feel.

For you, as a Christian, this is your faith and actions working together. You are doing the right thing while trusting God to do what you cannot do. Which is where step three comes in:

c. Affirm it

As you *admit* and take *action* to deal with your disconnection, God will give you grace to reach a point of closure. At that point you will have the joy of affirming your reconnection.

Go back to Thomas. He had to *admit* he was disconnected, then act in response to Jesus who gave him a personal opportunity to reconnect. The result was his declaration, *"My Lord and my God"* (John 20:28). He affirmed his reconnection.

Similarly, Peter had to admit his disconnection, act by staying close to Jesus and the disciples, and then in his grace Jesus created a moment for Peter to *affirm* his reconnection. He prepared a breakfast on the beach for him and gave him three chances to say he loved him to make up for the three denials (John 21:15-17). Jesus gave Thomas and Peter an opportunity to affirm their reconnection and he will do the same for you too.

So, keep watch over the soil of your relationships like a vigilant gardener. Looking out not only for the weeds we have identified in this book, but any small sign of disconnection. Then act promptly to deal with it.

2. Dig. The second practical thing all skilled relationship gardeners must do is to dig. When gardening, the digging usually follows the watching. We observe the need for soil to be turned over, weeds to be dug out, new stock to be planted, lawns to be aerated and so on. And out come the tools. However hard it is, digging is a non-negotiable when it comes to successful gardening. We must get the tools out, bend our backs and get stuck in. Lest that sounds a bit like hard work, let me remind you of something. All gardeners have a couple of tools they always have handy. Typically, something to dig with – a hand trowel, fork or hoe – and something to cut with, usually a pair of delightfully sharp secateurs. The vast majority of daily garden management jobs are completed using those basic tools. Only on special occasions do we drag out the large tools and our power-driven garden "toys". Most things just need a little clip, a little dig and our willingness to get our hands dirty.

Now that sounds simpler doesn't it? Yes, you will have to dig and get your hands dirty if you want to grow healthy relationships, but it is much easier when you have a few appropriate tools and use then regularly.

We established at the start of this book that God has made us social and spiritual beings. So the tools we need reflect this. They are spiritual tools for relationship building. And they are simple, if will just trust God and do things his way.

Sadly, people tend to overcomplicate relationship issues and the "soil" gets clogged, leading them to believe they need to get the spiritual rotavator out to deal with it – whereas in reality a hand fork will do.

So, what simple but effective tools has God given us for this purpose? Here are two indispensable ones: repentance and forgiveness.

a. Repentance

Repentance means to change your mind, turn, and go in the opposite direction. It is what the Prodigal Son did in the parable Jesus told (Luke 15). He came to a point where he recognised his error, was remorseful and decided to go back to his father. Then he actually got up and went. That is a cameo of repentance. All the intention in the world to fix the relationship meant nothing until he got up and went.

The Bible has lots to say about this simple process. It is a foundational teaching (Hebrews 6:1-3) and one we never move on from, just go deeper into. As Christians we live a "turned life" because we have repented from our old life to live God's way. That takes a daily decision to walk with God, be led by the Holy Spirit and take bold, faith-filled steps.

And when it comes to dealing with relationships, we repent often. We have a relationship ethic which says, "I repent" – we turn from the wrong towards the good, from doing it our way to doing it God's way – which always enriches the relationship.

b. Forgiveness

Forgiveness sets you free. Forgiveness is a choice to forget about something the other person did to you and to move on. It draws lines, brings closure and prevents bitterness building up inside you. It heals you. The other person benefits too, because they now know you are not holding the issue against them. A basis for relationship restoration is therefore achieved.

Many think forgiveness is all about the other person, but in reality it is mainly about you. Your forgiving them does not prevent them having to deal with the consequences of their actions. It does not "let them off" or let them "get away with it". We are each responsible for our words and actions and God will be the one who rewards us accordingly in this life and the next. No, forgiveness is firstly about *you*. It sets you free from the pain, the hurt and the anger. To be forgiven by someone is wonderful, but to be able to forgive is better.

These two spiritual tools work together in the teaching Jesus gave us about relationship restoration. He set two scenarios before us. In one, you are the offender, the bad guy. You have done something to damage a relationship – it could be anything. What are you to do? Jesus says:

"Therefore, if you are offering your gift at the altar and there remember that your brother has something against you, leave your gift there in front of the altar. First go and be reconciled to your brother; then come and offer your gift." (Matthew 5:23-24)

It is clear. You, the offender, take the initiative. That means you will have repented and will seek the forgiveness of the other person.

The second scenario Jesus gave reverses the situation. This time, you are the victim. Your friend or partner has offended you by doing or saying something and the relationship is damaged. It is without doubt their fault. So, what are you to do? Do you wait for them to read Matthew 5 and come and seek you out? You may have a long wait! Do you hold the moral high ground attitudinally and keep them at arms length until such time as they acknowledge their sin? That would be the temptation. But Jesus said, *"If your brother sins against you, go and show him his fault, just between the two of you"* (Matthew 18:15).

It is equally clear. Once again, you have to go and seek them out and make moves towards a reconciliation. Placing these two instructions together creates the culture Jesus is looking for in relationship restoration. He wants us to be proactive in the repair and restoration of our damaged relationships, whichever party we are. Ideally, we should meet each other on the way to see one another!

When this happens, relationships do not stay damaged for long. But it demands a commitment to using the two spiritual garden tools of repentance and forgiveness by everyone in the relationship.

How willing are you to bend your back and dig out anything that threatens to damage your primary relationships? It will require humility, grace, stature ... and getting your hands dirty!

3. Feed. Watching leads to digging, as explained. But alongside them the third action of the skilled relationship gardener is to consistently feed the relationship.

I believe that the majority – and maybe all – relationship issues can be prevented if we will regularly nurture the soil of our primary relationships with the nutrients we have identified in this book.

Recently, I visited the Garden Centre to replenish my fertilizer and feed supply. It is not as easy as you might expect. For a start, they are available in a range of forms: liquid, powders, pellets or organic manure. Which is best? Then, I discovered that there are a great many specialist feeds – more than I had previously realised, now that I was looking more closely. Some promote flowering, others foliage. Some suit acid soils, others more alkaline ones. Some are primarily one mineral or element – like potash or seaweed – and others are compounds made up from all manner of ingredients. There is one for roses, one for cacti, one for flowers, one for shrubs and trees, another for houseplants, and yet more for every variety of vegetable imaginable. And so we could go on. Suffice to say, I came away rather poorer than I expected because, after all, every plant needs feeding!

My point being that no one thing will supply the required feeds to keep the garden of your relationships healthy. It takes, at the very least, the fifteen ingredients we have identified earlier in this book.

If they were available in a box, all ready for you to apply, the ingredients list would read as follows:

1. Commitment to partnership
2. Personal health and wholeness
3. Good communication
4. Being trustworthy
5. Keeping good company
6. Resolving issues
7. Vision
8. Fun
9. Passion
10. Healthy compromise
11. Prioritising quality time
12. Self-control
13. Humility
14. Releasing
15. Wisdom

Make these you goal. Not only will they target the specific relationship weeds we identified, they will keep your relationship soil fertile, healthy and productive.

Pottering

A day rarely goes by when I don't walk into my garden just to enjoy it. I savour the fragrances, absorb its beauty and relax in God's marvellous creation. I am there for pleasure, not to work in it.

Then I spot a greenfly on a rose bud, so nip to the shed for insecticide and quickly spray it. As I continue to stroll I observe a dead head, so nip it off. Further along the path, the small shoot of a weed catches my eye, so I reach down and tease it out gently. I notice slugs have nibbled my Hostas, so back to the shed I go for slug pellets and pop them on the surrounding soil. Then I remember, it's time to feed the tomatoes, so quickly mix up some feed and pour it on. Before I know it, I have done all kinds of small maintenance jobs.

"What have you been doing?" asks Kay as I re-enter the house.

My reply: "Just pottering."

I love to "potter". In this context it means to move slowly whilst dabbling with things along the way. Much pottering is unintentional; we do it instinctively, on the hoof, or in the moment just because it comes to our notice as we wend our way through life. And I am a potterer!

My challenge to you is to become an intentional "relationship garden potterer". As you move through the various relationships in your life, keep your eyes open and do the little things as soon as you see them.

Watch, dig and feed as you go.

By so doing, you will keep the soil of your relationships fertile. And, as the seed – the "message of God's kingdom" – is sown in your soil, it will produce a harvest of wonderful relationships to enrich your life and fulfil you as the social and spiritual person God created you to be.

I pray that you will have the skill and wisdom to be a relationship gardening expert.

As for me, I'm off to potter in the garden.

References

The following are references used in the writing of this book. Some are directly quoted or mentioned whilst others are helpful, supporting resources.

Communication: Key to Your Marriage, H Norman Wright, Regal Books, 1974.

More Communication Keys for Your Marriage, H Norman Wright, Regal Books, 1983.

The Marriage Book, Nicky & Sila Lee, Alpha Publications, 2000.

The Peacemaker – A Biblical Guide to Resolving Personal Conflict, Ken Sande, Baker Books, 2004

How to Have That Difficult Conversation You've Been Avoiding, Dr John Townsend, Zondervan, 2005.

Boundaries, Dr John Townsend & Dr Henry Cloud, Zondervan, 2004.

The Sixty Minute Marriage, Rob Parsons, Hodder & Stoughton, 1997.

The Sixty Minute Family, Rob Parsons, Lion, 2010.

The Five Love Languages, Gary Chapman, Northfield Publishing, 1995.

The BEST Marriage, Anthony Delaney, The Message Trust, 2012.

Further Information

For details of other teaching resources and the ministry of Stephen Matthew please visit:

website: www.stephenmatthew.com

twitter.com/stephenmatthew_

facebook.com/pastorstephenmatthew

Life Church, Bradford: www.lifechurchhome.com

Other Books by Stephen Matthew:

Building Church (River Publishing, 2012)

Abundant Life Skills: a series of practical Bible study guides for personal or group use. Titles currently available:

Battle for the MIND
Bringing the BIBLE to Life
MONEY Matters
Increasing PEACE